The Palmistry Textbook

An Illustrated Guide to Reading Hands

**Text & Illustrations
by
Peter Burns**

The Palmistry Textbook
An Illustrated Guide to Reading Hands

© 2011 by Peter Burns

First Edition

Illustrations by Peter Burns
Book Design by Molly A. Sullivan
Cover Design by Molly A. Sullivan

International Standard Book Number: 9781934976340

Library of Congress Control Number: 2011940490

Published by Starcrafts Publishing, an imprint of Starcrafts LLC
334-A Calef Hwy., Epping, NH 03042
http://www.astrocom.com
http://www.starcraftspublishing.com

Printed in the United States of America

The Palmistry Textbook

**An Illustrated
Guide to
Reading Hands**

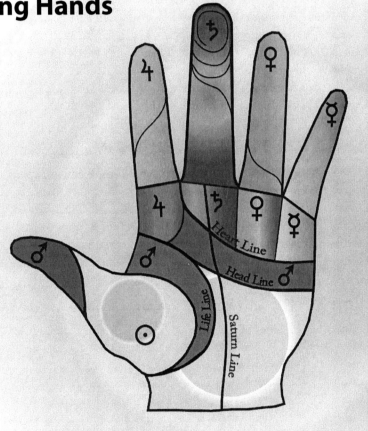

Peter Burns

Contents
The Lessons

The Illustrations

Preface

The aim of this book is to provide an up-to-date book on palmistry that brings it out of the dark ages of confused symbolism and misunderstood relationship with astrology. Palmistry is the 'poor cousin' of astrology. Astrology has a much wider appeal and has a broad international community of practitioners and researchers whose efforts continue to advance our understanding of the Art.

By comparison, the number of professional palmists is few in number and the opportunities for networking and coordinated research is minimal. Moreover, palmistry is saddled with a misappropriated symbology and a misunderstood relationship with astrology.

Basic relationship of palmistry with astrology

The basic relationship of palmistry with astrology is that the hands reveal which aspects of the horoscope are manifested in real life. An astrologer can spend hours studying a client's horoscope, but only when the client's hands are examined will the astrologer know which facets of the horoscope are actualized in the client's life. The connection between astrology and palmistry is the focus of my next book: *Astro-palmistry*.

Astrologers with knowledge of palmistry who wish to assess the future effects of important planetary transits and other cycles can use the timing mechanism provided by the hands to assess and correlate these cycles.

Rectification of misappropriated symbology

In regards to misappropriated symbology any competent astrologer will tell you that art, music, pleasure, beauty, presentation, and theatricality belong to the realm of Venus. However, in palmistry, there is confusion because the name Apollo, the Sun god of Hellenistic fame who was associated with the arts, was given to the ring finger. However, the distinction between Apollo as the deity ruling the arts and the Sun, which is the giver of life, has become blurred in recent times. The unfortunate result is that the ring finger has become associated with the Sun.

Likewise the name Venus, with its obvious associations with passion, has been given to the mount on the palm whose meaning most closely resembles that of the Sun. The Sun is associated with vitality, life, enthusiasm, motivation, and vigour. Passion is a necessary component of these qualities and it is not inconsistent to include it as part of the meaning of this mount. However, with the inclusion of the solar attributes of vitality, enthusiasm, and motivation, the true meaning of this vital area becomes apparent. That part of the hand which has traditionally been called the "Mount of Venus" actually belongs to the Sun.

When the Sun is assigned to the base of the palm beneath the thumb we see the two 'lights', the Sun and the Moon, sitting at the base of the hand, with the remaining traditional planets having rulership over the fingers and thumb. The luminaries power the hands and inform the meaning of the hands.

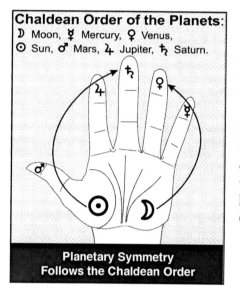

Chaldean Order of the Planets:
☽ Moon, ☿ Mercury, ♀ Venus, ☉ Sun, ♂ Mars, ♃ Jupiter, ♄ Saturn.

Planetary Symmetry Follows the Chaldean Order

Beautiful symmetry

With this insight the beautiful symmetry and underlying structure of the hands is revealed. Moreover we find that this symmetry is in accord with the ancient Chaldean order of the planets which is defined by their orbital periods: Moon, Mercury, Venus, Sun, Mars, Jupiter, Saturn. On the hands the Sun at the base is followed by Mars (thumb), then Jupiter (index finger) then Saturn (middle finger). Adjacent to the Sun is the Moon and the Chaldean order is followed back through Mercury (little finger) to Venus (ring finger).

Four different levels of interpretation

There are four different levels of interpretation which are integrated in this book. The first is the underlying structure which is defined and categorized by hand shape. The second is the genetic component as revealed by the dermatoglyphics which are the skin ridge engravings on the palm and the print on the fingers. The third is the zones and mounts of the palm which define the quality and type of energy within the palm. The fourth and final level is the lines of the palm which link these underlying three levels together and also provide a method of timing life events. In order to provide a flow of information that is easily assimilated by the beginning student I have included the genetic level last.

The primary aim of this text book is to provide students with no experience in palmistry with all the knowledge that is necessary to practice as a professional palmist. This knowledge is especially applicable to astrologers because of the reasons outlined above. However, a working knowledge of palmistry is also especially useful to those in the healing and helping professions, such as teachers, counsellors, nurses, and psychologists.

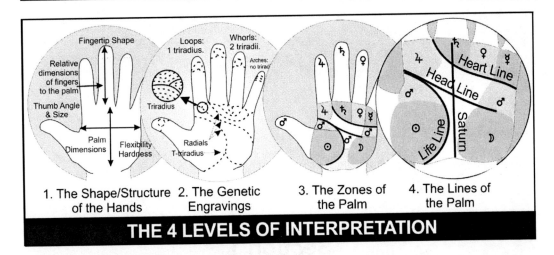

1. The Shape/Structure   2. The Genetic   3. The Zones of   4. The Lines of
   of the Hands   Engravings   the Palm   the Palm

THE 4 LEVELS OF INTERPRETATION

Quick and accurate diagnosis

The hands are without peer in the diagnostic professions for the ability to quickly and accurately diagnose and assess personality and its dysfunctions. Everyone carries with them two readily available maps of the psyche, one revealing their inner world and the other showing how these inner needs are met. The hands are unclothed and most cultures allow the hands to be examined.

In my personal experience of reading the hands of over 10,000 people since 1984 I am constantly amazed at the extraordinary personal insights revealed by the hands. This book is organized in a logical fashion, beginning with the basics and moving to the particular. Many students rush to examine the chapters about the lines of the palm, but without an understanding of the context provided by hand shape the real meaning will be missed. Good students will read the book from beginning to end.

An important feature of this book is that questions are provided at the end of each chapter to test your understanding. This book is like a mini-course where you have the opportunity to assess whether you have really understood the contents.

It is my intention to follow this publication with the results of my research in a future book on astro-palmistry. I wish you well in your studies.

Section 1

The
Master
Information

Lesson 1
Requirements to be a Hand Reader

Ethical Purpose

The most ethically correct purpose for reading the hands is to stimulate the client's self understanding and decision making in order to encourage, enable, and empower the client towards a more fulfilling future. The client's welfare is the first and most important priority, and everything else must come second to this, including the hand reader's need to make a living.

There is often a strong client expectation that you will tell their future. Ideally you will have communicated to your client what exactly you do and what you do not do before your client arrives, so that there are no awkward moments.

Fortune-Telling

The discussion of ethics leads us into the area of fortune-telling. Telling someone's future is likely to predispose them to fulfill the prophecy, because clients tend to believe what the reader says and unconsciously organise their lives in expectation of the prophesy's fulfilment. This does not allow for free choice/free will or the possibility of self development and personal improvement. To predict the future as something that is 'set in stone' and predetermined without the possibility of change can sow the seeds of destruction, and is morally questionable. The same can be said if hand reading is for the purposes of entertainment or ego building.

The practice of fortune-telling from the hands is based on the belief that the lines are set and will not change. This is quite incorrect. The lines can and do change, sometimes recording successful adaptations, and sometimes recording failure and disease.

However the hands do describe the parameters of what is possible. They show the basic nature and the limits of what is possible lie within the structure of this basic nature.

The lines of the palm can be understood to represent the belief system, at least on the sub-conscious level. When the belief system, which includes mental attitudes and emotional expectations changes, so do the lines on the palm.

Speak the client's language

It is very important to be able to communicate your message in a way that your client can understand. While you will use the insights gleaned from your interpretation of your client's hands to 'speak their language', it is important to have some natural skills in this area.

To be able to communicate your message in a way that your client can understand you must be adaptable, as no two clients are the same. You will use all your life experience to do this.

Listening skills

In order to assist clients you must be a good communicator. To be a good communicator you must be able to listen. The ability to listen requires alertness to your client's subtle (and sometimes not so subtle) messages. The ability to really listen, to listen deeply and sensitively, is vital to your success as a hand reader.

Assertiveness/interventionist skills

It is also important that you are able to intervene and assert yourself so that you can communicate your message and observations at important moments during the consultation. Allowing the client to ramble on endlessly does not necessarily provide them with the best service.

It is important to have a measure of control during the consultation so that you have time enough to both listen to your client's needs and impart your message. After all, the client is paying you for your insights.

Training

Yes, training in listening and communication, such as counselling skills, can be invaluable. So can self development courses and other endeavours which raise our awareness of ourselves and stimulate our desire to improve our capacity to live fully and with fulfillment.

However, to be a successful hand reader you do need some natural communication skills. Generally most beginning practitioners of the art of hand reading need to develop either listening skills or assertiveness skills. Most of us are endowed with one of these skills and need to develop the other.

Detached participation

During a consultation it is important to be fully involved in the interaction and also to be an observer of the interaction with yourself and the client at the same time. Yes this can be a challenge and does take practice and awareness. Ideally these 2 modes: full participation and detached observation, happen simultaneously.

Again most hand readers are good at one mode and need to develop the other. Full participation with the client enables the logical and intuitive faculties to be fully engaged. Detached observation provides a broad perspective of the interaction between you and your client. This broad perspective enables the hand reader to assess and understand the dynamics of the interchange, and to direct the process of the consultation towards a satisfactory conclusion.

The broad perspective includes an understanding of each stage of the consultation: the warm up phase, the discovery phase, and the wrap-up and enabling phase. These 3 phases of the consultation will be discussed in greater detail at the end of the course.

Resources, Beliefs, Ethics

It is important to have a well rounded and up to date understanding of available therapies, and the causes of those symptoms which reflect blocked energy, such as disease, failure, stress, and fear. Available therapies include both conventional and alternative and each has their place depending on your client's circumstances and belief systems.

Likewise an understanding of what promotes success, inner peace, good health and aliveness is essential. The practitioner's personal experience and success in overcoming difficulties will be an invaluable aid.

It is very important to be very self aware of one's own preferences, assumptions and belief systems, so that these are not imposed or projected onto the client. Training in counselling skills is particularly useful.

The most important attribute necessary for the practice of hand reading is the ethical requirement to make the best interests of the client a priority at all times. Nothing less will do. Sometimes this will mean that you do not conduct a consultation. When ethics are combined with competence there is the basis for excellence in the art of hand analysis.

Lesson 2

Historical Context and Terminology

The exact origins of palmistry are no longer known, although the use of identical terminology to astrology suggests that ancient practitioners were adept at both arts.

The history of palmistry goes back some thousands of years. Tradition has it that palmistry has been practiced in India for over 3000 years, although this is difficult to verify. As the practice goes back before written records the precise origins of hand reading remains a mystery.

It is reported that traces of chiromancy can be found in the Kabbalah, and that chiromancy was practiced by the Chaldeans, Egyptians, and Hebrews of ancient times. Palmistry has been practiced throughout Asia for centuries.

In the west we do have the records of Aristotle, Democritus, Artemidoris and Anaxagoras. The ancient Greeks were actively engaged in chirognomic research. The Middle Ages saw a demise of the arts of astrology and palmistry in the West, which coincided with the rise of modern science, materialistic and mechanistic thinking.

Since the 19th century, palmistry has gone through a resurgence throughout the Western world, popularised by Cheiro (Lord Louis Hamon) and others at the turn of the twentieth century.

In Asia and the West, astrology and palmistry have often been practiced together. Until the Middle Ages, a competent and experienced astrologer would normally consult the hands for verification and expansion upon what is shown in the astrological chart.

While the study of astrology has been popularised in recent decades with the advent of the 'modern psychological' model, and more recently with the resurgence of traditional astrology, palmistry has lagged behind to become the poor cousin.

Modern hand analysis offers an exceptionally quick and detailed method of understanding the way humans think, feel and act. It also provides an understanding of basic motivations, life strategies and dysfunctions. Each person carries with them two maps of their psyche, on which are recorded the effects of the past, adaptations and strategies for survival.

In more recent times over the last 3 decades there has been considerable research by the universities and the medical profession into the dermatoglyphics on the fingers and the palms. The dermatoglyphics are the skin engravings, commonly referred to as fingerprints when found on the finger tips.

These engravings are found all over the palm side of the hands and reflect our genetic endowment. This new contribution to the store of knowledge by the medical profession does not take into account the context of hand shape or even recognise the insights of palmistry, and consequently it is an isolated although valuable study.

Chirognomy and Chiromancy

These two terms refer to two different branches of palmistry.

(i) **Chirognomy** refers to the study of a person's character using the shape of the hands. This practice was in wide use in ancient Greece.

(ii) **Chiromancy** refers to the fortune-telling aspects of palmistry using the line and markings on the hands. This practice has traditionally been most common in Asia, particularly on the Indian sub-continent.

In more recent times these two aspects of palmistry have been combined. With the advent of psychological perspective last century, palmistry has taken on a new role: that of identifying the psychological make-up of a person through the study of the hands.

Names: Palmistry, Hand analysis, Chirology

Technically the name "palmistry" is a misnomer as it suggests that only the palms are studied.* "Hand analysis" is a more accurate term. "Chirology" (chiro = hand, -ology = study) is also a very accurate term although most people do not recognise the name. For convenience we will continue to use the name "palmistry."

Palmistry and Astrology

When combined with astrology, hand analysis provides a comprehensive life picture, enabling the consultant to more accurately evaluate overall life direction and the impact of important transits. Consulting astrologers who also understand the basic principles of successful hand reading are able to provide a more accurate interpretation, and thus offer more benefit to their clients.

The exact origins of these sister arts is no longer known. Whether or not they actually had a common origin is also an unknown fact. However we have inherited a map of the hands which uses astrological terminology which suggest that there is a long history of practitioners using both techniques together.

Whatever the historical origins, the most important connection for the present day practice between palmistry and astrology is quite fascinating: **The Hands Reveal The Manifested Horoscope.**

The hands record how the horoscope works, and what the individual brings into reality from the horoscope.

There are many different ways in which the potential shown in the horoscope can be manifested. Social attitudes, gender, geography, and historical situation are only some of the variables that can influence the expression of the horoscope's potential. The hands show what the individual makes of this potential in terms of psychological make-up and direction in life. This is the real connection between astrology and palmistry.

There is a further advantage to astrologers in learning palmistry. In many cases it is difficult for astrologers to assess exactly which aspects of the client's life will show the effects of major transits. However the lines of the palm can be accurately dated and the hands will show which area of the person's life will come under the spotlight at the age indicated by the astrological transits.

*This information is invaluable to any serious astrologer.

Questions to Test Your Understanding
(see Page 154 for answers)

Are the following statements true or false?
1. Chirology is the study of Chiron the centaur, known to some astrologers as the 'wounded healer'.
2. Chiromancy is the study of the lines of the palm.
3. Chirognomy is the study of the face.
4. The hands show which elements from the astrological template are expressed.

Lesson 3

Hand Shape—the Key to Interpretation

The Structural framework

Most new students of palmistry are very eager to learn about the lines of the palm, but do not realise that the meaning of the lines depends so much on the context of hand shape and structure. Consequently one of the major themes of this book is about putting things in context. In order to accurately interpret the hands, we must first know their structure.

The structure of the hands is like a container and describes the basic nature. This is the bedrock which provides the meaning for all other features.

The structure of the hands shows how to interpret the lines, and the lines show how the energy of the structure is processed. Thus the meaning of the lines is intimately connected to the type of structure on which they are found.

The structural framework of the hands is revealed firstly by the shape and relative proportions of the hands, and secondly by other factors such as flexibility, refinement, hardness and thickness.

This framework shows basic needs and lifestyle preferences. Although we can categorise structural frameworks into many types, they can be distilled into four basic types, or combinations of these four types. These are: activity, physical expression, thought and emotions. These four types relate to the three basic human activities: action, being, thought and emotion.

Later in this course these four basic hand types will be described in more detail, but for the moment interpreting other features within their context will demonstrate one of the most important skills required in hand analysis: interpreting combinations of features.

An understanding of the structure also informs the reader about how to relate and communicate with the client. For example, if the hand structure of your client indicates a sensitive emotional person whose greatest need is to express feelings and to nurture others, then it is pointless speaking about purely career and factual matters, when relationships and feelings are what most concerns them. Alternatively if the hand structure suggests a strong intellectual bias, then a logical and reasonable approach needs to be taken if there is to be a rapport with your client.

I have spoken with a number of hand readers with strong philosophical views who have expressed frustration dealing with clients who have elementary, basic and earthy hands. Clients with this hand type are unlikely to be receptive to any philosophy and will seek out the advice of a palmist only in the most desperate circumstances. They are not seeking intellectual inspiration but rather practical solutions in a time of crisis.

It is so important to be sensitive to the needs of the client. The hand shape and structure will indicate the needs of the client.

These examples are used to indicate the importance of understanding hand structure. The context given by the framework of the hands gives meaning to the type of energy being transmitted by the lines of the palm. Understanding hand structure is not very difficult, but does require some time and practice.

The lines of the palm

The lines of the palm show how the structure is expressed. They show how different parts of the psyche are linked together. The lines tend to follow typical patterns common to each of the four basic hand types.

To interpret the lines without reference to the structure is not very smart. Something of the process represented by the lines will be understood, but without an understanding of the context from which the lines take their meaning, the interpretation is likely to be superficial at best.

It is common, even normal, for those beginning the study of palmistry to have a fascination with the lines of the palm. This is OK if this study then continues to include the context in which the lines are found.

Questions to Test Your Understanding
(see Page 154 for answers)

Are the following statements true or false?
1. The lines of the palm have exactly the same meaning on all hands.
2. The lines of the palm should be read within the context of the hand shape.
3. The meaning of the lines of the palm changes according to longitude.
4. The hand shape is determined by the length of the Life Line.
5. The meaning of the hand shape is reversed for people living in the southern hemisphere.

Lesson 4

Which Hand do I Read?

The short answer is that you must read both hands. To read only one would be to tell only half the story. One hand will reflect your external world, and is sometimes called the 'outer', 'dominant' or 'active' hand. In this book it will be referred to as the 'outer hand'.

The other hand reflects your inner world, and is often called the 'inner' or 'passive' hand. In this book it will be referred to as the 'inner hand'.

How can I tell which is the outer hand and which is the inner hand?

It is very important to establish at the beginning of a consultation whether your client is right or left handed. Many of your interpretations will be based on this information. If your client is right handed, this is the outer hand, and the left hand is the inner hand.

The reverse is true if for a left-handed person, when the left hand is the outer hand, and the right hand is the inner hand.

Many people will explain that they are partly ambidextrous, preferring one hand over the other for different tasks. Keep it simple – in almost all cases you can safely identify the hand the client writes with as the outer hand.

In some earlier generations it was common for teachers to force children who are naturally left handed to write with the right hand. If you were a natural left hander who was forced to change, then your left hand is the outer hand.

If you are uncertain, then the hand you write with is usually your outer hand. If you are still uncertain look to see which hand is slightly larger? The larger hand will be the outer hand.

On an anatomical level the hands reflect the two hemispheres of the brain. The brain is divided into two halves, each specialising in different functions. Although each hemisphere is capable of performing most functions, one hemisphere deals more with logic, spatial and mechanical activities, and the other deals more with intuition, feeling, and communication. These two hemispheres are normally contra-lateral, which means that each reflects the opposite side of the body. The right hemisphere of the brain operates the left side of the body, and the left hemisphere operates the right side of the body.

It has become popular in recent years to describe people as 'right brained' or 'left brained', a reference to whether someone is guided by intuition (right brain) or logic (left brain). However there is considerable cross-over and it is a mistake to assume that either hemisphere has exclusive dominion over logic or intuition. In hand analysis the left hand reflects the right hemisphere, and the right hand reflects the left hemisphere of the brain.

What is the meaning of the inner and outer hands?

The hands provide two maps of the psyche which together form a complete picture. These maps are two interlocking perspectives of the same person. To use the musical analogy: one hand gives the words or melody, the other the harmony, and together they make the music.

The inner hand reveals the private life and inner world of feelings, wants, desires and needs. The outer hand reveals the public life, the 'outer persona'.

The outer hand reveals the 'life strategy' for satisfying the inner needs. This 'life strategy' is not normally thought out in a logical or reasoned fashion. It generally has its genesis in the infant years when life had different priorities and when adult reasoning was not fully developed. Compensations for lack of love and affection as well as strategies for gaining love and acceptance are shown in the outer hand.

The outer hand reveals the outer personality, career and public presentation, as well as involvement in the professional world of business and career. The inner hand reveals the inner and private world, and the domestic experience as well as relationship life.

The Sun and the Moon

In astrology the Sun and the Moon are viewed as a pair. The bright light from the Sun pours out and is reflected by the Moon. The Sun represents the rational mind and the Moon represents the emotional mind. The Sun relates to the conscious ego and the Moon to the unconscious. The Moon is the beloved partner of the Sun, waxing and waning with his light, filling up and then emptying out. She represents the emotions, the feelings and desires which come and go.

So it is with the hands. The inner hand is the Moon hand, showing the unconscious needs and desires, the need for relationship and the emotional nature. The outer hand is the Sun hand, showing the outward behaviour, strategies and social presentation. Together they make music, with the Moon providing the harmony and the Sun the words. The inner hand shows the wants and desires and the outer hand shows how the needs are realised.

The symbol for the Sun is the circle of spirit with the point of individuation at its centre. The Moon is shown as a crescent, like a receiving dish.

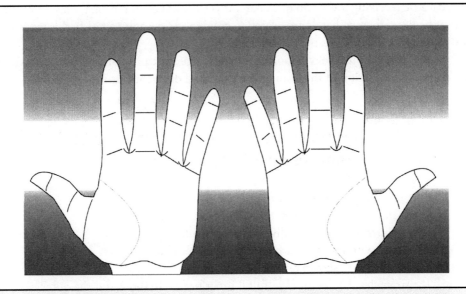

Inner Hand (yin, Passive)	Outer Hand (Yang, Active)
Inner wishes	Survival stategies
Domestic environment	Coping behaviors
Unconscious motivation	Conscious action
Relationship needs	Outer behavior
The Moon	**The Sun**

Handedness: Inner & Outer Worlds

What is the difference between the inner and outer hands?

It is the difference between the two hands which is important and which provides deep insight into personal motivation and life scripts. The most obvious difference is when each hand has a clearly different shape, although this is not common. However there is often a slight difference in hand size.

A more common difference is shown in finger length, which can reveal personality differences in areas such as assertiveness at home and at work, and communication abilities in the domestic and the work environment. Differences in finger tip shape, fingerprints and finger bends will also be important, as are other minor features.

It is very common to find important differences in line structure between the two hands. Differences between the two hands do not generally show a 'split personality' in the modern pathological sense. Rather differences show adaptations to environmental conditions and challenges.

The challenges which can have a most profound effect, and which can be identified on the hands, relate to the need to feel loved and accepted in the infant and developing years. The hand analyst who is able to accurately read these indications is in a good position to provide valuable insight and perspective to the client.

Because receiving love from one's parents is such a basic and primary need, most of the differences between the two hands are related to childhood attempts to satisfy this requirement, and are expressed in later life as personality traits.

In the next chapter we will look at the basic structure of the hands and how this provides a key to interpretation of the lines of the palm and different features of the hands.

Questions to Test Your Understanding
(see Page 154 for answers)

Are the following statements true or false?
1. The hand you write with is normally the outer hand.
2. The smaller hand is normally the inner hand.
3. The hand with the longest fingers is the outer hand.
4. Career is mostly shown on the inner hand.
5. The strategies that are used to fulfill inner needs are shown on the outer hand.

Lesson 5

Hand Structure

The hand shape as a mirror of consciousness

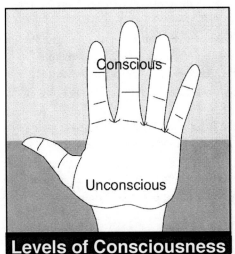

Levels of Consciousness

The shape of the hand reflects the model of consciousness used in many popular psychology courses. This model uses the shape of a pyramid to represent the mind.

The tip of the pyramid (like the tip of an iceberg) represents the conscious mind. The next layer beneath represents the sub-conscious mind, and the lower area represents the unconscious mind.

The shape of the hand reflects this model: the fingers represent the conscious mind, the upper palm represents the sub-conscious mind, and the base of the palm represents the unconscious mind. The base of the palm also represents the mind of the body, sometimes called the "body mind" or more humorously "the beast within" - that part of us that yearns for physical satisfaction, often in spite of our best logic.

On a simpler level the fingers represent the mind – specifically the conscious rational and adult mind, and the palm represents the 'body-mind', the less conscious and more childlike part of our nature. Hands with very long fingers compared to the palm show that the rational adult mind dominates. Hands with a very large palm compared to the fingers show that the instincts rule.

The 4 quadrants

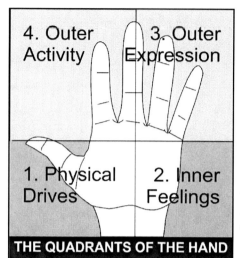

4. Outer Activity

3. Outer Expression

1. Physical Drives

2. Inner Feelings

THE QUADRANTS OF THE HAND

For the purpose of understanding the meaning of the different parts of the hand including the lines, the hand can be divided into four areas. These four areas are the combination of a vertical division of the hand and a horizontal division of the hand.

The vertical division is indicated by an imaginary line drawn from the middle of the wrist through to the middle of the tip of the middle finger. The area on the thumb side of the hand reflects involvement in the outer world of physical and social activity. The area on the little finger side of the hand is associated with the inner world of emotions and fantasies.

The horizontal division shown by a line is drawn from the middle of the upper palm area above the thumb across to the percussion side of the palm. The area incorporating the base of the palm represents the inner unconscious drives and emotions, and the area incorporating the fingers represents the expression of these drives and emotions in the outer world.

The *Physical Drives Quadrant* comprises the area at the base of the thumb, and represents the physical drives, such as the need for exercise, sex, and sensual satisfaction in its different forms.

The *Inner Feelings Quadrant* comprises the base of the palm beneath the little finger, and reflects emotional needs, as well as the sense of mystery, creativity and imagination.

The *Outer Expression Quadrant* comprises the Mercury and Venus fingers and the upper palm beneath them, and is associated with the expression of the inner feelings in a social context.

The *Outer Activity Quadrant* incorporates the Jupiter finger and the upper palm beneath it, and is associated with the execution of wishes and desires and the assertion of inner needs in the outside world.

The names of the four quadrants are self-descriptive and need to be memorised. The meaning of the lines, mounts, zones and fingers can be better understood when viewed from their placement within these four quadrants.

The direction of energy flow

The basic energy flow within the hands, which reflects the energy flow within the psyche, rises from the wrist through to the tip of the fingers, and from there into the outer world. From the base to the top is the basic rule. The exception is the Life Line, which can be read in either direction and has a different meaning according to the direction being considered.

General Overview

The two most basic components of the hands are the left and rights hands.
One level below this is the palm and fingers.

So far we have covered the 'Master Information' relating to the meaning of the left and right hands and to the four quadrants. Next we will look at the meaning of the palm and fingers, and other important features relating to hand structure.

An understanding of this 'Master Information' is vital to the understanding of what follows in this book. I understand that most students want to skip this information and rush on to the chapters covering the interpretation of the lines. This is understandable, but unless the hand structure is well understood, the ability to interpret the lines of the palm will be diminished.

Combining Handedness with Quadrant meanings

When the left and right hands show a difference in development, with one hand showing an area that is larger or smaller than the other hand, then there is a structural difference between the hands. A structural difference suggests something which is very important because it is basic to the functioning of this individual.

For example, if the *Outer Activity Quadrant* shows a disproportionate development compared to the *Inner Feelings Quadrant* on one hand, but this is not seen on the other hand, then there will be difference between motivation and action. If this is the case in a right-handed person where the disproportionate development of the *Outer Activity Quadrant* occurs in the left hand, the implication is that this person is motivated by the need to achieve success/leadership in the outer world. If this disproportionate development of the *Outer Activity Quadrant* occurs in the right hand, then the interpretation would be that this person fulfils their needs by through leadership in their field of chosen endeavour.

If it is the heel of the hand, *Inner Drives Quadrant*, that is comparatively large compared to the other quadrants on the right hand of a left-handed person, then it is the inner emotions and irrational forces such as anxieties or creative imagination which motivates behaviour.

Identifying Unusual Features

As a general principle we can say that the unusual development of any feature of the hands reflects a person who does not conform to social 'norms'. This unusual development may be a feature which is minimised (unusually small) or maximised (excessively developed). Unusual hand features can include any part of the hands including quadrants, fingers or lines on the palm. Unusual development of any hand feature will set this person apart and 'make or break' them; or at least play a major part in their success or failure.

It is also most likely that unusual features will be the primary contributor to most problems experienced by a client. If someone with unusual hand features presents as a client I suggest you explore the meanings and consequences associated with the unusual feature and encourage the client to talk about these matters so as to develop strategies for success.

An unusual feature found on one hand only will reflect a difference between the private (inner hand) and public (outer hand) life of this person. Your skill at combining the meaning of inner/outer to the meaning of the unusual feature will contribute to success at gaining a client's confidence and contribute to your competence as a hand reader.

Questions to Test Your Understanding
(see Page 154 for answers)

Are the following statements true or false?

1. The *Physical Drives Quadrant* reveals the strength of the emotions.
2. The top of the hand reveals the most conscious part of the psyche.
3   The *Outer Expression Quadrant* records the ability to express feelings and ideas in a social context.
4. As a general principle, energy flows from the base to the top of the palm.
5. When one hand quadrant is disproportionately large, it reveals dyslexia.

Lesson 6

Palm Dimensions

The palm represents the physical drives and the emotional nature. This follows one of the least stated axioms in palmistry: that the higher the placement of any feature on the hand, or the higher the placement of any feature on any part of the hand, the more conscious is the awareness relating to the meaning of that feature. The lower any feature is placed on the hand or on a part of the hand, the more the meaning of that feature can be described as basic and unconscious.

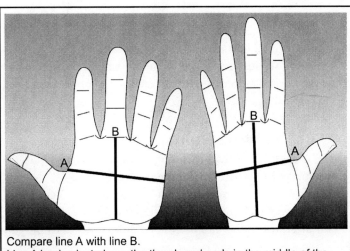

Compare line A with line B.
Line A begins just above the thumb and ends in the middle of the outer edge of the palm.
Line B links the middle of the wrist with the base of the Saturn finger.
In the palm on the left line A is longer than line B.
Therefore this is a wide palm, sometimes called broad or square.
In the palm on the right line B is longer than line A.
Therefore this is a narrow palm, sometimes called long or slender.

Measuring Palm Width

The palm, and particularly the lower palm, represents the unconscious side of our nature. It contains all the physical yearnings and desires. It contains our emotional and other primitive drives.

Hand shape shows how we deal with life at a basic level. Simply put, broad palms (also described as square or wide palms) indicate an outgoing nature in a physical and social sense. Here awareness is focused on the external world.

By contrast a narrow palm, which can also be called 'slender' or 'long' , indicate a nature that is turned inward, with awareness focused on inner thoughts and emotions.

If you want to become a good palmist, do not gloss over this section. It is the foundation for all that follows. If you think you know it already, read it anyway. Your thinking may be further stimulated. These relative dimensions of the palm are part of 'the master information', and must be understood clearly. The word 'relative' is the key here.

Terminology

A couple of basics on terminology: a square palm is a broad or wide palm. A square palm is as wide as it is long. A very broad palm is wider than it is long, although this is relatively uncommon.

A narrow palm, which is longer than it is wide, is also sometimes called a long palm or a slender palm. The words narrow, long and slender can be used interchangeably. Don't get confused!

Palm Dimensions:

The length of the palm is measured from the bottom of the middle finger at the webbing in a vertical line to the centre of the base of the palm. The width of the palm is measured from just above the thumb in a horizontal line across to the other side.

When the vertical measurement exceeds the horizontal measurement the palm is considered long. When the horizontal measurement equals or is longer than the vertical measurement, then the palm is considered wide.

The Meaning of the Wide Palm

When the palm is wide as or wider than it is long, then the focus is upon the external world, with the need to become active in that environment.

The basic need is to do things with a purpose in mind. A very wide palm shows that the outdoors has a strong appeal. The broad palm gives a more expansive feel to life than a narrow palm. It indicates practicality and a sense of order. This is an outgoing person in the physical sense.

Extra width to the palm endows its owner with more competence and capacity to handle the practical issues of life. If the palm is well padded then this person will also be outgoing in the social sense.

The Meaning of the Long Palm

When the palm is longer than it is wide the basic need is to express something. If the long palm is soft to touch then the need is to express emotions. This interpretation is reinforced if the soft palm also has some padding, which adds to the depth of emotional expression.

However if the long palm is firm or feels hard, then a hard and tough approach to life is taken. Firmness condenses and locks in the emotional energy and directs its expression through physical or mental channels.

If the long firm hand is also flat then there is little emotion or friendliness to be expressed, resulting in a physical or mental approach to life.

It is important to distinguish between the long palm which reflects the need to express emotions and the long palm which shows the need to express ideas. The emotionally expressive hand is long, soft and has some padding. The intellectually expressive hand is hard, flat (little padding).

Long palms show a person motivated by the needs of their inner world. Self reflection and introspection is indicated by the long palm. A very narrow palm suggests a tendency to be hesitant and withdrawn. This person is more likely to seek an indoors life focused on self centred activities.

Variations on the Shape of the Palm

There are 3 basic variations on the broad and narrow palm shapes already described, which will allow you to modify your reading.

1. The palm which is broader at the base and narrower at the top:

When the lower palm is disproportionately developed, then there is strong development of the unconscious and physical drives. This palm shape reveals powerful physical drives. The base of the palm is the "motor" of the hand, and when it is enlarged, the physical drives are powerful. The fingers and thumb, as well as the quality of the lines, will how these forces are activated.

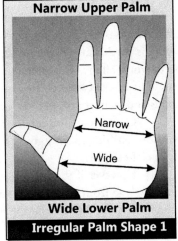

Narrow Upper Palm

Narrow

Wide

Wide Lower Palm

Irregular Palm Shape 1

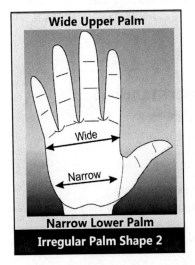

Wide Upper Palm

Wide

Narrow

Narrow Lower Palm

Irregular Palm Shape 2

2. The palm which is broader at the top and narrower at the base:

Here the meaning of the upper palm gives the clue as to which quality is strongly developed.

The upper palm represents the mental and higher emotional energies of the body/mind. This palm shape shows that it is the mental energy which is the driving force behind life's activities. Satisfaction is derived from mental pursuits. This hand shape shows a very active mind at work.

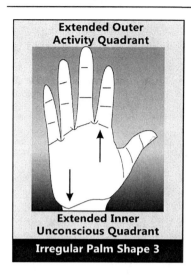

Extended Outer Activity Quadrant

Extended Inner Unconscious Quadrant

Irregular Palm Shape 3

3. The irregular palm shape

Here the base of the palm is dropped low on the *Inner Feelings Quadrant*, and the upper palm is elevated on the *Outer Activity Quadrant*. This irregular shape reflects a life expression which is more extreme and unpredictable. This person can be very logical and ambitious in an outer-worldly sense some of the time, and emotional and irrational at other times.

The strong development of the the *Inner Feelings Quadrant* reveals a strong development of the inner unconscious forces of the psyche, emphasizing the unconscious and irrational side of the psyche.

The upper and outer side of the palm, the *Outer Activity Quadrant* reveals a powerful and conscious need for active assertion in the outer world. The conscious awareness of outer reality is particularly emphasised, reflecting a strong desire for competence and effectiveness in outer world affairs. This irregular palm shape shows that the foundation of the personality is in a state of flux between consciously directed outer world activity, and the expression of unconscious and irrational directives.

On a broad and muscular hand this fluctuating expression will take on a physical expression, pushing this outgoing social person into more extreme forms of behaviour, usually on the social periphery.

However if the palm is narrow and soft to touch, then it is the expression of feelings which will go from one extreme to another, sometimes rational, and sometimes irrational. If the palm is firm and narrow and the fingers knotty, then it will be the intellect that dominates, with a shift in the expression of ideas and belief systems from one extreme to another, sometimes rational, and sometimes irrational.

Questions to Test Your Understanding
(see Page 154 for answers)

Are the following statements true or false?
1. A wide palm is longer than it is wide.
2. A narrow palm shows the need to express feeling and/or ideas.
3. The length of the palm is measured from the base of the Saturn Finger to the base of the palm.
5. A wide palm shows the need for purposeful action.

Lesson 7

Finger Length

We now move from the palm, which represents the unconscious, to the fingers, which represent the conscious mind. The fingers show how the energy contained in the palm is expressed through the mind. The energy that rises from the palm is divided into four channels. Each channel reflects a particular development and specialisation of the basic human drives which are represented in the palm, and these channels represent different functions of the mind.

The fingers (and the upper thumb) enable the articulation and application of the comprehension that arises through the feelings. The fingers show the ability to live in the present. Together, the fingers show the ability to relate to the past by screening memories through the mind and comparing them with the present.

If there are any significant anomalies in the fingers, the ability for objective understanding of the feelings is reduced, and the objective appreciation of memories is also diminished.

Measuring the Length of the Fingers

The golden rule is:

The Fingers Are Always Measured Relative To The Palm.

The fingers are long, medium, or short.

Always use the middle finger as your measurement for overall finger length.

Measure the fingers from the back of the hand.

If the fingers are only as long or shorter than the palm, then they can be considered short. If the fingers are longer than the palm, they are long.

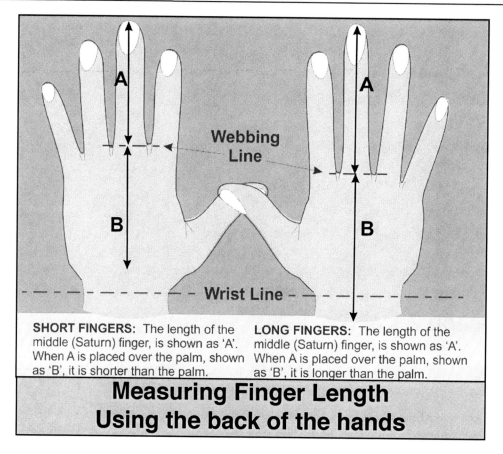

SHORT FINGERS: The length of the middle (Saturn) finger, is shown as 'A'. When A is placed over the palm, shown as 'B', it is shorter than the palm.

LONG FINGERS: The length of the middle (Saturn) finger, is shown as 'A'. When A is placed over the palm, shown as 'B', it is longer than the palm.

Measuring Finger Length
Using the back of the hands

In the graphic above, Line A on the left hand measures the middle finger from the tip to its base. Its base is taken as the beginning of the webbing.

Line B is exactly the same length as Line A. It is drawn from the base of the middle finger down to the wrist. The wrist on the back of the hands is at the same level as the top rascette line on the palm side of the hand. The rascettes are the lines that divide the wrist from the palm.

Line B, which is the same length as Line A, does not reach the wrist line. Therefore these fingers can be classified as short. In the hand on the right, Line B goes past the wrist line. The length of the fingers exceeds the length of the palm. Therefore the fingers are long.

If you find finger length difficult to measure you are in good company as most students new to palmistry find it challenging. It is perhaps the most difficult aspect of palmistry to learn. My suggestion is to just keep practising. Gradually your eye will tell you whether the fingers are long or short without measuring.

The Beginners Trap:

Fingers often appear longer on a long palm even when they are actually short. And on broad palm fingers often appear shorter than they really are. For these reasons it is important to actually measure them.

The following text describes fingers as either long or short. This description of finger length extremes is useful for understanding the meaning of finger length.

In practice

However, in practice, fingers can be long, medium long, medium short or short. More often fingers fall within the medium description, either medium long or medium short, in which case you will need to moderate your comments concerning length as described below. Nature does not always comply with our request for clear cut measurements.

The Meaning of Short Fingers

As the fingers represent the mind, and are channels for the thoughts to flow through, short fingers do not allow thoughts to stay in the mind very long. Thoughts spend less time in the brain and rush through very quickly. Thus short fingered people think quickly and want to do things very fast. They are less 'full of thought' (thought-full) than long fingered people, and are more intuitive and emotional.

Short fingered people are excellent at grasping the overall picture, and become impatient with detail.

Short fingers emphasise the overall perspective and the holistic view.

People with short fingers like to talk in broad terms, and rely more on intuition than detailed logic. They are quick at grasping the essential points of a topic.

Short fingers on wide palms

Wide palms show the capacity to comprehend the broad vista, and cover many subjects. Short fingers on a broad palm show a quick instinctive response.

Short fingers on narrow palms

On a narrow palm the mind takes on more specialised viewpoint, and short fingers show a quick response within the boundaries of this specialised viewpoint.

The Meaning of Long Fingers

Long fingers show that the thoughts spend a longer time in the brain. The thought processes are therefore extended, and more time is allowed for consideration and deliberation. The brain structure permits more detailed thinking, and the thinking process is enjoyed for its slowness.

Thus, long fingered people have an excellent grasp of detail. They are more thoughtful and introspective. These people have a good ability to finish things.

Long fingers on wide palms

If the palm is wide, then there is a practical and purposeful foundation for this detailed thinking. These people often make good administrators and organisers.

Long fingers on narrow palms

If the palm is long and soft, then there is a lot of thought given to feelings and the expression of feelings. These people can be very introspective and emotionally expressive.

If the fingers are long and the palm is hard, then it is the intellect that rules. These people often are excellent communicators.

Finger Outline

When the joints of the fingers appear to stand out they are described as "knotty". These fingers bulge at the sides where the joints are located.

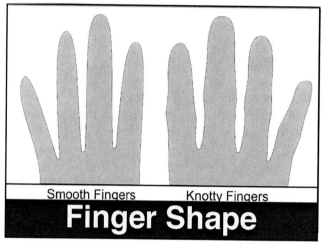

Smooth Fingers   Knotty Fingers

Finger Shape

When there is no bulging at the sides the fingers are described as "smooth". Remember that the fingers represent the mind. As the energy passes through the fingers, it is slowed down by knotty joints, and passes unhindered when the fingers are smooth.

Smooth fingers indicate that the passage of thought through the fingers is unimpeded by analysis which is represented by the joints. Smooth fingers show an intuitive approach to life.

The slowing down of the passage of thought by knotty joints results in analysis and detailed thinking. Thus people with knotty fingers can be described as analytical and detailed in their thinking process.

There are three sections on each finger, and two joints between these three sections. The lower joint represents matters relating to the more practical affairs of life, and the upper joint refers to theoretical matters. Normally it is the lower joint which is knotty. It is rare to find the upper joint also knotty.

When both joints are knotty, the there is a pronounced emphasis on analysis and detail. The mental process is slowed down for the careful consideration of minutiae. This is a sure indication of the analyst who will go to great lengths to consider every angle. This person will enjoy the slowness of the process of theoretical abstraction.

It is important to take into consideration here whether the fingers are long or short compared to the palm. We can combine finger length with the qualities of the finger joints to produce the following combinations:

Combining Finger Outline with Finger Length

Combining the qualities of different traits is one of the most important skill requirements for the hand analyst. In this case we are combining the qualities of short fingers with either smooth or knotty fingers, or combining and long fingers with either smooth or knotty fingers. This produces four possible variations:

1. Short and knotty fingers.

This person is a quick but careful thinker. The big picture is grasped quickly and particular points are analysed quickly.

2. Short and smooth fingers.

The qualities relating to short fingers are exaggerated. This person has a fast intuitive mind and is impatient with detail, and needs to be able to comprehend the big picture quickly in order to make sense of life. The hand structure will describe what underlying needs are seeking expression.

3. **Long and smooth fingers.**
   Intuition is combined with thorough and deep thinking. This combination is very common. People with these fingers can be described as "thoughtful and intuitive."

4. **Long and knotty fingers.**
   Analysis is combined with a love of detail. This person enjoys careful and slow consideration without reference to how long the process takes. Pedantic is a word often used to describe these people. There is absolutely no point trying to hurry them. The word "hurry" is not in their dictionary! If the fingertips are square these characteristics will be exaggerated further.

Questions to Test Your Understanding
(see Page 154 for answers)

Are the following statements true or false?
1. Long and knotty fingers show a love of detailed analysis.
2. Short and smooth fingers show emotional inhibition.
3. Long and smooth fingers show a combination of intuition and deep thinking.
4. Short fingers reveal a practical mind.

Lesson 8

Hand shape—Combining Palm and Fingers

In Chapter 6 the shape of the palm was discussed, including the two basic varieties of broad palms and narrow palms.

In Chapter 7 finger length and shape was discussed.

When the two basic palm shapes, long and broad, are combined with the two basic variables of finger length: long and short, the result is four basic hand shapes. Following is a brief summary of these four variables:

Broad (wide) palms: Outgoing in a physical and/or social sense, needs action with a purpose.
Narrow (long) palms: Need to express the inner world either through feelings or the mind.
Short fingers: Quick thinking, big perspective, intuitive.
Long fingers: Slower detailed thinking.

These four variables form the basis of understanding hand shape, and should be committed to memory. When these 4 variables are combined they form the 4 basic hand shapes which reflect the 4 elements of fire, earth, air and water commonly used by astrologers:

Fire Hand: long palm and short fingers.
Earth Hand: Wide palm and short fingers
Air Hand: Wide palm and long fingers.
Water Hand: Long palm and long fingers (hand must be soft and supple).

Unfortunately the outline which corresponds to the Water Hand can be misleading. In astrological parlance 'water' corresponds to emotion. However a hand with this outline is only a Water Hand if it is also soft and supple. If a hand with this outline is firm and inflexible and also has knotty fingers, then it is the mind that dominates, not the emotions; in which case we would describe it as 'the philosophical hand'.

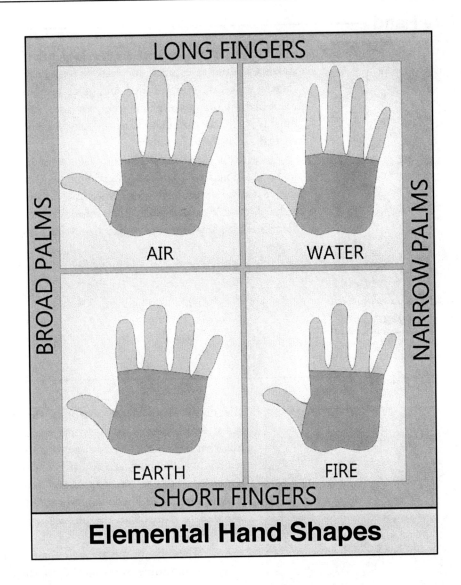

Astrological Correspondence

While these 4 shapes are very useful, their two dimensional description does not include a number of important variables found in real life: hardness/softness, flexibility, skin texture, finger smoothness and finger tip shape. Sometimes our neat schemes do not always match what is found in real life! However they are useful as a starting point for analysing hand shapes. As we move through the book we will look at more sophisticated models.

Aside from this notable exception of the Water Hand, these 4 hand outlines reflect the 4 astrological elements very well. This is not to say that hand shape always corresponds with the Sun-Sign element. It does not. As any competent astrologer will tell you, the Moon sign and the sign on the Ascendant and the qualities of the Ascendant ruler can often mask the Sun sign.

The Fire Hand

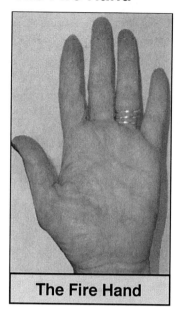

The Fire Hand

The Fire Hand shape combines the long palm, which shows the need to express emotions or ideas, with short fingers, which show an intuitive and quick response. This combination shows someone who expresses themselves quickly and without deliberation. They are often described as 'fiery and impulsive'.

It is more common for the palm of the fire hand to be thick and well padded, showing a depth of feeling. It is also important to assess whether the hand is soft or hard, flexible or inflexible. These other characteristics describe the many different variations of this basic hand shape.

The hands on the left belong to a very intuitive person.

The Earth Hand

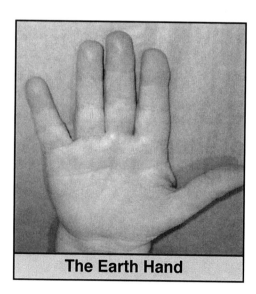

The Earth Hand

The Earth Hand shape combines the wide palm, which shows an outgoing nature focused on the external environment, with short fingers, which show an intuitive and quick response. This combination shows someone who is practical and has a natural and intuitive response to nature and the physical environment.

These hands are generally hard, muscular, and inflexible, showing the capacity for hard work and stamina, combined with fixed attitudes and responses. Generally there are few lines on the palm showing a strong preference for a simple and uncomplicated lifestyle. With more lines, softness or flexibility, other variables are introduced which will incline the person to more social involvement and intellectual sophistication.

The Air Hand

The Air Hand shape combines the wide palm, which shows an outgoing nature focused on the external environment, with long fingers, which show a thoughtful approach. This combination is frequently found on administrators and executives who combine a practical awareness with the ability to organise and regulate.

Hands with this shape are generally firm and have moderate flexibility, and medium-long fingers. Other variations on this shape such as softness, flexibility and coarse skin will inform your personality description.

The example on the left clearly shows the very long fingers on a wide palm.

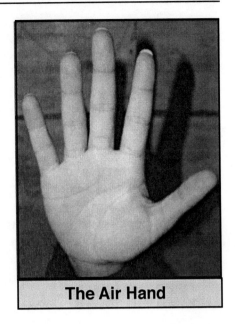

The Air Hand

The Water Hand

The Water Hand shape combines the long palm, which reveals a focus on the internal world of thoughts and feelings and the need to express these inner experiences, with long fingers.

As described above, for a hand with this outline to qualify as a Water Hand it must also be soft and supple. In this course I have also described this hand as 'the sensitive emotional hand'. This combination of softness and suppleness plus the introversion revealed by the narrow palm shows a very sensitive and emotional person. The internal world of feelings colours all perceptions and life is defined in terms of what they 'love'.

They have a remarkable ability to care and nurture others, and to adapt to the needs of others. It is common for people with sensitive emotional hands to think that people who disagree with their opinion don't like them.

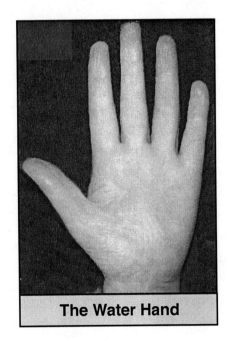

The Water Hand

The hand with long fingers on narrow palms shown in the above photograph is a good example of a Water Hand.

The Philosophical Hand

When the water hand shape is found on a hard inflexible hand, the narrow palm shows introversion and specialisation, and the long fingers show thoughtfulness. On this hand shape the fingers are always knotty and the palm is usually flat. This hand has often been called " the philosophical hand". People with these hands have little capacity for emotional expression and tend to specialise in intellectual pursuits or sales, or as trades people where their motor skills enable them to excel. They are often excellent communicators. This hand shape will be discussed more fully in later chapters.

Questions to Test Your Understanding
(see Page 154 for answers)

Are the following statements true or false?
1. Fire hands have long fingers.
2. Water hands have broad palms.
3. Earth hands have broad palms.
4. Air hands have long fingers.

Lesson 9

The Finger Tips

The overall shape of the hands reflects the shape of the body in the sense that the palm symbolises the unconscious 'body-mind' and the fingers represent the conscious mind. This principle is based on the model of consciousness outlined in Chapter 5.

The higher any feature is located on the hands or on a section of the hands, the more that feature represents a higher level of consciousness. Following this reasoning a step further: the tip of the fingers reflects the higher mind, and in particular the way that the mind organises the thinking for its expression into the outer world. The shape of the finger tips reveals how a person acts and communicates.

Below are described the basic finger tip shapes. Frequently finger tips are a blend between 2 types, and it is necessary to blend the meaning of different features. The most common finger tip type is the rounded finger tip. The pointed and square finger tip types are less common, and the spatulate type, which might be considered an unusual development of the square finger tip, is quite rare.

For a quick guide to the finger tips use the thumb, as it is generally a good representative of all the finger tip shapes. It is quite rare to find a significant difference between the 2 hands, although minor differences will be observed.

A more detailed examination will often reveal a variety of finger tip shapes, but with little variation between them. Generally the Jupiter (index) and Mercury (little) fingers are more conical on a hand where rounded finger tips dominate. On such a hand the Saturn finger tip is usually slightly squarer, and the Venus finger has a slightly more spatulate appearance. However the differences are usually quite small.

Please note that it is very difficult to show finger tip shape by looking at hand prints. Often the nails distort the outline image and sometimes the fingertip outline is not drawn correctly.

Pointed Finger Tips

How to identify

Fingers taper towards the nail phalange making them look pointy.

Meaning:

Pointed finger tips express a speedy passage of thought which is expressed as impulsiveness, spontaneity and idealism. Activity and expression is not hindered by methodical reason. Pointy fingers permit a free flow of dreams and feelings from the psyche into the outer world. These finger tips are often found on the natural psychic and on those who appreciate the unconventional.

People with pointed finger tips are receptive, impulsive, idealistic, sensitive, impressionable, dreamy, and often have a love of music and the arts. However they are impractical.

When found on thick powerful hands with coarse skin, this feature will show a love of speed based on the use of power, and is often found on those who are labelled as "petrol heads". These are people who love racing or driving powerful motor vehicles. If the lines on the palm are few and broken, there may be a tendency to impulsive violence.

When found on soft slender and refined hands, pointed finger tips indicate the dreamy romantic inspired by love, poetry and soft music.

On hands showing a strong aptitude for skilful communication, this pointed finger tip shows an unconventional intelligence combined with a sharp verbal response. On the philosophical hand, pointed finger tips amplify persuasive abilities. Pointed finger tips are most common on long soft slender hands, which indicate a receptive, emotional and idealistic person.

Conic Finger Tips

How to identify:

Fingers taper towards the nail phalange, but to a lesser degree than pointed finger tips.

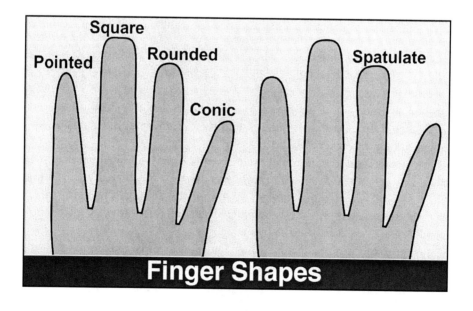

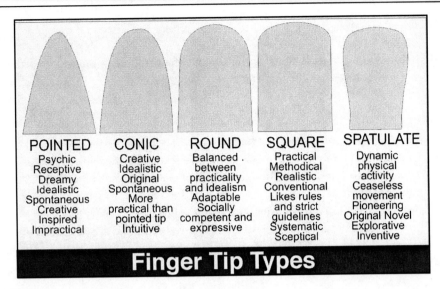

POINTED	CONIC	ROUND	SQUARE	SPATULATE
Psychic	Creative	Balanced .	Practical	Dynamic
Receptive	Idealistic	between	Methodical	physical
Dreamy	Original	practicality	Realistic	activity
Idealistic	Spontaneous	and Idealism	Conventional	Ceaseless
Spontaneous	More	Adaptable	Likes rules	movement
Creative	practical than	Socially	and strict	Pioneering
Inspired	pointed tip	competent and	guidelines	Original Novel
Impractical	Intuitive	expressive	Systematic	Explorative
			Sceptical	Inventive

Finger Tip Types

Meaning:

Conic finger tips show some impulsiveness and dreamy idealism, similar to those with pointed finger tips, but with more practicality. There is a greater emphasis on the functional aspects of life.

However these people are still somewhat unconventional and impulsive, but not as idealistic and dreamy as those with pointed finger tips. When found on hands showing indications of leadership and strong will power, both the pointed and conic tips indicate a softer and less severe approach to others than people with square and spatulate finger tips.

Square Finger Tips

How to identify:

Fingers maintain the same width from base to tip. The tip looks flat compared to other finger tips.

Meaning:

Square finger tips show systematic and well ordered thinking, with an emphasis on practicality, regularity, structured thinking, and rational methodical decision making. A strong sense of method pervades the mind. These are generally conservative people who like to follow convention and protocol.

The square tip holds back the energy which rises up through the fingers so that its spontaneous expression is restricted and moulded into a systematic methodical process. These people are well suited to occupations requiring adherence to structured rules and regulations, such as the military services. This finger tip type is also very common amongst tradesmen and occupations where tradition and adherence to time-honoured principles is important.

Square tipped fingers are most often found on hands with broad palms.

Rounded Finger Tips

How to identify:

The nail phalange tapers a little towards the tip and the tip looks more rounded than square finger tips but less pointy than conic finger tips.

Meaning:

Rounded finger tips reveal a blend of idealism and practicality. These people have 'common sense'. Adaptability and competent expressiveness is indicated by these finger tips, assuming the rest of the hand indicates nothing to the contrary. People with rounded finger tips comprise the majority of the population. They are able to work with a sense of method and logic, as long as it is "rounded out" with some inspiration and comic relief.

However rules and regulations which are excessively rigid will not be tolerated for long. Some sort of sensitivity and inspiration must be incorporated into their daily life if they are to feel fulfilled.

Spatulate Finger Tips

How to identify:

Spatulate finger tips look like the top finger section is swollen, resembling a doctor's spatula.

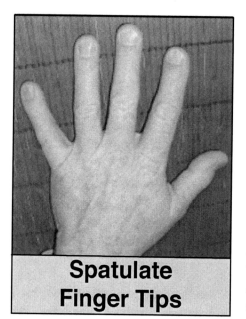

Spatulate Finger Tips

Meaning:

This is the rarest finger tip type. The shape of these fingers reveals that the energy of the psyche is driven outwards in dynamic activity.

These people need action and movement. Their sense of order is imbued with an originality of expression. Original and novel methods appeal to these people. People with these tips are renowned for their explorative and inventive natures. They relish the establishment of new enterprises and ventures.

Look to the overall structure of the hands to see how this dynamic activity will be expressed. On broad thick hands with coarse skin there will be a love of sports and physical pursuits in general. These people will go crazy if kept indoors for too long.

Combined with hand shapes

On the firm thin intellectual hand spatulate finger tips indicate prodigious output and energetic pursuit of knowledge, such as studying, research and lecturing. This might also be the 'irrepressible salesperson' whose energetic persuasion can drive people to distraction.

On the sensitive emotional hand spatulate finger tips are very rare. This rare combination will indicate dramatic emotional expression, requiring some fulfilling outlet such as the stage and theatre. However this hand shape shows little control and the presence of spatulate finger tips would suggest the possibility of emotional burnout.

When spatulate finger tips are found on a Fire Hand it shows a very dynamic person, in which case the rest of the hand needs to be checked to establish whether dynamic activity can be sustained. However spatulate finger tips on a Fire hand are quite rare.

Questions to Test Your Understanding
(see Page 154 for answers)

Are the following statements true or false?
1. Square finger tips look flat at the tip.
2. Spatulate finger tips have a pointy appearance.
3. Round finger tips appear to swell on the nail phalange.
4. Conic finger tips taper towards the tip.
5. Spatulate finger tips appear to swell on the nail phalange.
6. Pointed finger tips appear flat at the tip.

Lesson 10

Additional Features Relating to Hand Structure

The relative dimensions of the palm and fingers, including the various components of the fingers outlined in previous lessons, are like the skeleton of the body. They support and define its parameters.

Other qualities, such as the musculature and skin refinement, describe this structure and give it life and character.

Do not underestimate the importance of these additional qualities. Although each is described separately here, and seems obvious and simple enough once explained, your understanding of how they combine will determine the accuracy of your overall reading.

It is important to spend time looking at as many hands as possible, and studying how these hand features describe their owners. Comparing many hands will provide a mental database for accurate assessment.

Most of the features described in this chapter cannot be measured with a ruler. You will need to use personal judgement, which will be based on your experience of examining and comparing many hands.

Padding

Padding refers to the fleshy bumps or mounts on the palm of the hand (hills and valleys). This is the musculature of the palm. These mounts have been given individual names, such as the Jupiter mount, the Saturn mount, etc. Each mount has its proper (or normal) place on the palm, and each has its own meaning. The individual meanings of each will be described in a later chapter. For the moment we are concerned about the general picture.

Look to see whether the palm has lots of bumps. Compare your hands with the hands of many other people. This comparison will give you perspective on which hands are well padded and which are flat. As always there will be many hands that fall between these two extremes. Thick hands generally have more padding and thin hands have less padding.

The meaning of Padded hands

Padding indicates outgoing emotional energy. It shows warmth, friendliness and an active and outgoing disposition. On a broad palm this padding shows an outgoing nature in both the physical and social sense. Broad well padded palms are very common, particularly on men. Normally this combination is expressed as warmth and friendliness.

On a narrow well padded hand, the energy is expressed in a more restricted or specialist environment. This shows a powerful focus within a smaller range of personal interests, backed up by strong emotional content. If the hands are also soft, emotions will be readily expressed.

The meaning of Flat Hands (lack of padding)

Flat hands (very little padding) show that there is little emotional energy available, indicating that the intellectual sensitivities dominate. Without the outgoing energy represented by the padding, the flat handed person is more reliant upon internal resources, and is more withdrawn.

If the palm is broad and flat, the natural outgoing nature takes on a more intellectual flavour, but without the camaraderie shown by the well padded hand.

If the flat palm is also narrow the person lives in the world of the mind. This may show the specialist. To determine whether this world is dominated by feelings or ideas we must look at the consistency of the palm (see below).

Flat hands with narrow palms are more common than flat hands with wide palms. On hands which indicate persuasive ability flat hands offer intellectual presentation.

Consistency - Soft or hard padding

Hardness and its opposite: softness, relates to the surface tension of the palm. Is the hand soft or hard to touch? As with all measurements this assessment is relative. Some hands are unusually hard and some are particularly spongy. Most hands fit somewhere in between. Generally hands are relatively firm or relatively soft. Only the experience of comparing a large number of hands will provide clarity as to which hands are hard and which hands are soft.

Soft hands

Soft hands show an emotionally expressive person. These people laugh and cry easily. Feelings and emotions are easily and readily expressed. This feeling energy is not easily transformed into physical energy, with the result that owners of soft hands are very economical about physical exertion, and consequently are frequently described as lazy. Their ability to nurture others and their ability to express feelings are their strengths.

Soft hands show someone who does not drive themselves hard in a physical sense. In regard to the disciplining of children or directing employees they find it very difficult to be hard and tough, and will instead prefer other methods of persuasion and control.

Hard hands

Hard hands show that the emotional energy is 'hardened' and is expressed as physical energy. In regard to the disciplining of children and directing employees they find it easy to be 'hard and tough' when the occasion requires. These people 'work hard' and contain their feelings.

Their feelings are expressed though a sense of togetherness with other people in a social context. Singing, music, community projects, clubs and sporting endeavours provide common outlets for their restrained emotional energy. In Western culture the feelings are commonly loosened by alcohol.

Hard hands usually show a preference for hard exercise and indicate 'locked in' mental and emotional attitudes. Their attitudes and opinions are less forgiving than people with soft hands

Flexibility

Bending the fingers back from the palm gives a quick indication of the overall flexibility of the personality, particularly the emotions. Each finger and thumb may also be flexed back to assess its flexibility.

Rigid hands are those which refuse to bend. Rigidity of the hands shows a rigid outlook upon life. This person is unbending, inflexible, and very controlled. Rigidity shows a locked in attitude that refuses to accept anything that is not understood. In times of stress these people tend to break or snap rather than adapt to change.

Supple hands

Very supple hands show a person who very flexible and pliant. This indicates little control, with the ability to adapt, but in the sense of going to extremes. On small well padded hands this suggests extravagance and generosity. Generally it shows difficulty in holding onto emotions (particularly when the hands are also soft) or money.

Most hands fall between these two extremes, in which case you would describe the character of the person as leaning one way or the other.

Flexibility of the thumbs

The thumbs show flexibility in attitude. A thumb which bends back past the 90 degree angle suggests a very open minded and generous person. A rigid thumb shows a closed attitude. If the fingers also show little flexibility and the hands are hard, the overall assessment is that this person is rigid, inflexible and controlled.

Skin texture

The texture of the skin (always use the back of the hand) indicates refinement in terms of sensitivity, taste in general, and lifestyle preference. Again this is one of those assessments that can only be done accurately when backed up the experience of reading the hands of many people. Age and weathering by the elements can complicate the assessment. A light touch on the back of the hands will generally indicate the level of refinement of the skin. The palm side of the hands is not generally used because the skin becomes rough in response to physical labour.

Fine skin

Fine skin shows emotional sensitivity and a preference for mental activity. Indoor work is preferred; especially if the palm is also narrow. Refinement will be expressed in art and décor, choice of clothing and speech, as well as choice of occupation and general attitude to life. People with fine skin are not known for swearing and prefer subtlety.

Coarse skin

Coarse skin shows strong physical drives, coarse and vulgar tastes, and a love of the outdoors. These people will easily swear, use foul language, and make crude jokes. They are very in touch with the physical aspect of life. Their choice in art is crude and earthy.

Palm Thickness

The depth of the palm shows the amount of energy that is stored in the palm, and therefore the amount of energy or stamina the person has at their disposal. Again this will normally reflect body shape. Thick hands are generally found on people who are wide and heavy. Thin hands are found on slimmer and thinner people.

To assess thickness: hold the middle of the palm between thumb and forefingers to gain an assessment of thickness. If your assessment takes longer than 10 seconds, then you are unnecessarily confusing the issue. Thin hands show little staying power. Thick hands show a lot of energy in reserve.

Hand Size

How to identify:

The ability to assess hand size comes with experience in comparing different hands. Generally large hands are found on large people, and small hands are found on small people. Seems obvious? However this is only a general rule.

Large hands

Large hands enjoy a slow and steady approach to life. These people are thorough, and have patience with detail. Large hands are usually found on larger people. Big hands on small people show an unusually dexterous and decisive person. These people are frequently found in the trades doing skilful manual or engineering work.

Small hands

Small hands show a quick and lively person, good at grasping the overall perspective. These people like the BIG picture. They are generally found on smaller people. Small hands on big people show the ability to combine steadiness and consideration with the ability to grasp the big picture quickly. This is a rare combination.

Temperature and Colour

How to assess:

These attributes are mentioned in the literature on palmistry but in real life their practicality is reduced by environmental factors such as the prevailing weather when outside and room temperature when indoors.

Temperature

The basic principle is that warm hands show warmth and generosity and have good health and circulation; Cold hands show coldness and meanness, and poor health and circulation.

This basic principle correlates with health. Those people with robust health are more likely to feel generous and passionate, while those with poor health need to conserve their energy and have less to offer.

Colour

Clearly colour is strongly influenced by racial factors.

Most of the available literature in the West is written by white Caucasians, and cannot be universally applied to people of all races. When applying these principles you must use discretion and sensitivity to racial differences.

Combined Meaning

The basic principle for white people is that pink-red hands which are also warm show good health and generosity, while cold hands which are also pale hands show coldness and poor circulation.

Generally pink-red hands are usually warm to touch, and pale hands are usually cold to touch.

Questions to Test Your Understanding
(see Page 154 for answers)

Are the following statements true or false?
1. Soft hands show emotional expressiveness.
2. Flexible hands show intellectual communication.
3. Padding on the palms reveals flexibility of mind and emotion.
4. Flat hands show that little energy is available for emotional expression.
5. Broad and flat hands shows a preference is for intellectual expression.
6. Padding on the palm shows intellectual energy.

Lesson 11

The Mounts and Zones of the Palm

Terminology

Most palmists speak of the 'mounts of the palm', even though there may not necessarily be a physical mount present. One example is the mounts beneath the fingers. A quick glance at the palm will show that the mounts on the upper palm are actually situated between the fingers, not below them (with the exception of the Jupiter Mount). Likewise the Mounts of Mars are rarely separate mounts. One is an extension of the Mount of the Moon, and the other is an extension of the Sun Mount. Thus I will refer to the so called mounts under the fingers and the Mars mounts as 'zones'.

The Zone of Mars on the little finger side of the palm, which is often called 'Upper Mars' in the books, shall be referred to in this course as 'Inner Mars', because it is on the inner side of the hand.

The Mars mount between the beginning of the Head Line and the thumb, which is often called 'Lower Mars' in the books, I shall refer to as 'Outer Mars', as it is situated on the outer side of the hand. The terms 'inner' and 'outer' enable you to easily locate and identify which Mars Zone is being discussed.

Where are the boundaries of the zones and mounts?

The zones of the upper palm are named after the fingers above them, and located between the relevant finger and the Heart Line (the upper transverse line) below. The boundaries between these zones are imaginary lines drawn from between the fingers directly down to the Heart Line below (see diagram).

The zones beneath the fingers energise and empower the fingers. They provide a power base (like a battery) for the expression of the qualities represented by the fingers. When these zones are flat the overall expression is intellectual rather than physical, technical rather than imaginative, and somewhat 'flat' in the sense of having little emotional content.

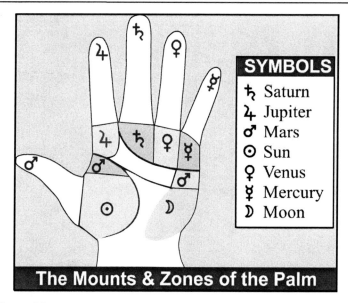

The Mounts & Zones of the Palm

The Jupiter Mount

The Jupiter Mount is the exception: it is usually an actual mount at the base of the Jupiter finger. It is located in the area beneath the Jupiter finger and above the Head Line. Its inner boundary is an imaginary vertical line drawn down from the gap between the Jupiter and Saturn Fingers.

The Saturn Zone

The Saturn Zone is the area directly beneath the Saturn Finger down to the Heart Line. It is bordered on one side by the Jupiter Zone and on the other side by the Venus Zone.

The Venus Zone

The area directly beneath the Venus Finger down to the Heart Line is called the Venus Zone, and is bordered on one side by the Saturn Zone and on the other side by the Mercury Zone.

The Mercury Zone

The area directly beneath the Mercury Finger down to the Heart Line is called the Mercury Zone, and is located on the edge of the palm adjacent to the Venus Zone.

The Sun Mount

Note that this mount has been traditionally called 'the Mount of Venus', but as any competent astrologer will tell you, art, beauty and sensuality are traits associated with the realm of Venus, not the Sun. Therefore I have renamed this mount the 'Mount of the Sun'. It is the Sun which provides our vital life giving energy and the Mount of the Sun is encircled and defined by the Life Line. Its size is defined both by the arc of the Life Line and its height. This is normally the largest mount on the palm. It is located in the Physical Drives Quadrant.

The Outer Mars Zone

The Outer Mars Zone is also defined by the Life Line, and its lower boundary is a horizontal line where the webbing of the thumb meets the palm. It is located in the Outer Activity Quadrant immediately above the Sun Mount.

The Mount of the Moon

The Mount of the Moon is the area at the heel of the hand opposite the thumb located in the Inner Feelings Quadrant. The size of the Mount of the Moon is shown by the height of the mount and its protrusion on the side of the palm. Its boundary on the thumb side of the palm is sometimes difficult to discern.

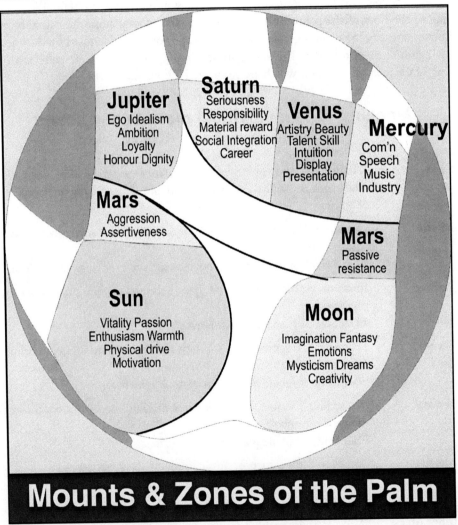

Mounts & Zones of the Palm

The Zone of Inner Mars

The Zone of Inner Mars sits between the Head and Heart Lines, and straddles the boundary between the Inner Feelings Quadrant and the Outer Expression Quadrant. The Plain of Mars is the valley in the middle of the palm.

The general meaning of the mounts and zones

The mounts (another word for padding) show outgoing energy - energy that is directed towards the outside world. They were discussed in lesson 9. In this lesson we will examine the mounts in more detail.

An absence of a mount will show the absence of the quality associated with that mount, and also a more inward turning nature if many mounts are absent.

Each mount or zone adds character, which in the outward expression its associated qualities.

Each mount/zone has a natural location on the palm, and if there is a shift from this position then the personality is shifted to a more extreme or unstable expression.

An understanding of the meaning of the zones and mounts is essential for an understanding of the lines of the palm. The lines derive their meaning from the way they connect the different areas of the palm together. The mounts and zones are energised by the lines of the palm which link them together. The key to understanding the lines of the palm is an understanding of the areas of the palm which are connected by the lines.

Meaning of the individual mounts and zones
Keywords for the zones of the palm

Sun: Vitality, vim and vigour, enthusiasm, motivation, passion, sensuality.
Flat: Lack of vitality, motivation and enthusiasm. Low sex drive. Withdrawn.

Moon: Emotions, imagination, fantasy, mysticism, dreams, creativity, travel, water.
Flat: Prefers routine to adventure, unimaginative, phobias, irrational anxieties.

Jupiter: Idealism, ambition, high principles, self-esteem, ego, pride, honour, dignity.
Flat: Low self esteem, the follower.

Saturn: Seriousness, responsibility, sobriety, material reward, career, wisdom study.
Flat: Lack of focus. Indifferent to achievement.

Venus: Art, beauty, pleasure, fun, style, presentation, intuition, recognition, vanity, forgiveness.
Flat: Sense of inadequacy.

Mercury: Communication, speech, music, industry, business acumen.
Flat: Inarticulate. Lacks expression. Finds it challenging to express feelings and ideas.

Inner Mars: Passive resistance, inner resilience, inner resolve and courage, devotion.
Flat: Cowardly. Little resolve to oppose injustice.

Outer Mars: Assertiveness, aggressiveness, urge to fight, competitiveness.
Flat: Easily offended by small slights but has little 'fight'. Irritable.

Notice that the keywords for each mount form a constellation of ideas. Each set has a common theme for which there is no single English language equivalent.

The Jupiter Zone is the only true 'mount' on the upper palm. The line which most often links up with the Jupiter Zone is the Heart Line. This shows high ideals and principles, and a heart which reaches out idealistically. Sometimes the Saturn line extends a branch to this mount. The meaning of the lines is discussed in the chapters dedicated to individual lines.

Questions to Test Your Understanding
(see Page 154 for answers)

Are the following statements true or false?
1. The Sun mount represents vitality and enthusiasm.
2. The Mercury zone is located adjacent to the Jupiter zone.
3. The Venus mount is associated with beauty, art and creative expression.
4. The upper mounts of the palm are located between the fingers.
5. The Mount of the Moon is located in the inner feelings quadrant.
6. The Mount of the Moon is associated with passion and feelings of confidence.

Section 2

The Fingers
and
Thumb

Lesson 12

The Meaning of the Fingers and Thumb

The fingers represent the mind, and show how the energy which arises from the unconscious mind is dealt with in real life. They show the ability to live in the present and to screen the memories through the mind so as to compare the past with the present. When finger length shows a significant departure from the 'norm' or when fingers have a significant sideways bend the individual leans towards more extreme personality expression, which can create difficulties with social integration.

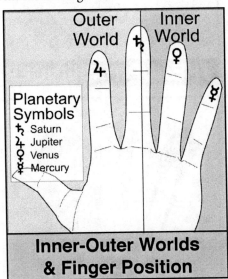

Inner-Outer Worlds & Finger Position

The diagram on the left shows the inner and outer divisions of the hand. From this we can see that the fingers on the thumb side of the hand deal with the outer external reality of our lives. These fingers are the thumb and the Jupiter finger. The outer world includes everything that is outside of us...the social and physical challenges and opportunities that we encounter in our everyday environment.

The fingers on the Mercury finger side of the hand deal with the inner subjective reality of our lives. This is the world of our inner needs, emotions, feelings, desires and fantasies. These fingers include the Mercury Finger and the Venus Finger.

The central finger, the Saturn Finger, balances the two sides of the hand (the two sides of the psyche). This finger symbolises our capacity to balance the demands of the inner and outer worlds. It is like the control centre which says what is allowed to happen and what is not allowed.

The Thumb

The thumb describes the will and focus of the personality. Its strength shows how the various drives and wishes are fulfilled and controlled. Because it occupies a unique position on the hand relative to the other fingers it will be discussed separately in Chapter 17.

The Jupiter Finger

The Jupiter finger is on the outer side of the hand, and therefore shows how we deal and interact with the outside world. This is the "executive" finger, indicating how we assert our will on the world around us.

The Jupiter Finger indicates our degree of confidence and assertiveness. It sits between the thumb, representing our willpower, and the Saturn finger, representing our conscience and sense of responsibility. The Jupiter finger reflects pride in oneself, self esteem, and the wish to manage others. It has been called the 'ego finger'.

The Jupiter finger's involvement in the activities in the outer world also is associated with its function concerning perception and observation. For example whorl fingerprints on this finger indicate intense and focused powers of observation. Fingerprints will be discussed in a later lesson. Of all the fingers, the Jupiter finger is most involved with conscious reality. Those with a strong Jupiter fingers on both hands will endeavour to impose their will in a social or physical context. To be effective this will MUST be backed up by a strong thumb.

The Mercury Finger

The Mercury Finger, which sits on the inner side of the hand, deals with the expression of the inner world of emotions. The Mercury finger shows how our inner needs, such as the need for communication and intimacy with others, finds expression.

The Mercury Finger reflects how we communicate in general. It covers a broad range of communication, including speech, writing, music and even business. This finger shows the power of negotiation and has a particular relevance to business activities.

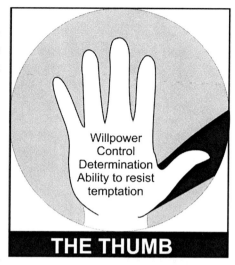

Willpower
Control
Determination
Ability to resist
temptation

THE THUMB

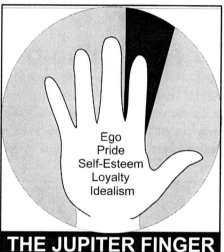

Ego
Pride
Self-Esteem
Loyalty
Idealism

THE JUPITER FINGER

Communication
Negotiation
Music
Speech
Business

THE MERCURY FINGER

In a basic sense the Mercury Finger shows how the energy of the libido is expressed, whether this be through the mind, emotions, music, business or sex. In particular the Mercury finger is involved with the expression of love and feelings of personal intimacy. We can call this 'communication finger'.

The Venus Finger

This finger has been traditionally called 'the Apollo Finger', but as any competent astrologer will tell you, art and beauty, the two traits most commonly associated with this finger, belong to the realm of Venus, not the Sun.

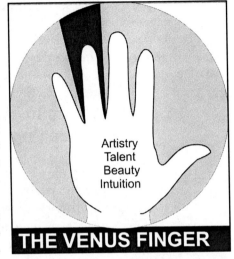

Taking the Saturn Finger as the dividing line between the inner and outer worlds, we can see that the Venus finger sits on the inner side of the hand, in the Outer Expression Quadrant, and therefore deals with the expression of inner needs.

As it sits between the Saturn finger, which represents conscience and internalised social standards, and the Mercury (little) finger which represents communication in all its forms, the Venus Finger shows how the inner needs find a social expression.

Traditionally this finger is associated with artistry and the expression of talent. However it does not indicate artistic ability per se, but rather is an indicator of the ability to make use of artistic talents. It is through this finger that the creative energies of the psyche find expression. Strong creative energies are shown by a well padded Mount of the Moon, and if this area is diminished, so is creativity, and therefore the Venus Finger will be unable to express creative talents, but will instead show technical skill and associated talents.

When the Venus finger is long it shows that the inner world and intuition is well developed, and also indicates a strong need for social recognition. A long Venus finger also shows a strong intuitive faculty and the capacity for emotional empathy when combined with a strong Sun mount.

The Saturn Finger

As this finger sits in the middle of the hand, it represents the balancing function of the psyche. It functions like an internal judge, and shows what we allow ourselves to enjoy. It shows our sense of responsibility and guilt when responsibilities are not fulfilled. It reflects the internalisation of the rules and standards we were brought up with, and dispenses pleasure or guilt in response to actions we consider permissible or forbidden.

The Saturn finger is also the tallest of all the fingers, standing above and looking down upon the rest. As such it represents the intellectual capacity to order and systemise. While this is not the same as reasoning ability (seen on the second section of the thumb), or the way in which intelligence is applied (the Head Line), its function is to endow the intellect with the capacity of understanding in order to balance to competing needs of the psyche.

This understanding leads to wisdom and the ability to deal with the real world. This finger has to do with our sense of reality and also with wisdom and understanding. Its meaning is similar to that given to the planet Saturn by astrologers.

In traditional palmistry this finger is associated with agriculture and farming, a pursuit that is now enjoyed by a small percentage of people in the Western world.

Questions to Test Your Understanding
(see Page 154 for answers)

1: Which fingers lie on the inner side of the hands?
2: Is the Mercury finger associated with artistry or communication?
3: Is the Jupiter finger associated with ego or emotions?
4: Is the Jupiter finger located on the inner or outer side of the hand?
5. Is it true that an unusually long Mercury finger is associated with someone who talks a lot?
6. Is it true that an unusually short Jupiter finger is associated with someone who feels superior?

Lesson 13

Measuring and Interpreting the Fingers

The fingers and thumb rise from the palm, linking together in intelligent movement. The palm describes the type of energy which powers the fingers. It is therefore important to be able to describe and interpret the main features of the palm. These include whether the palm is broad or long, soft or hard, thick or thin, large or small, and whether the skin texture is fine or coarse.

The meaning of the individual finger sections (called phalanges) will be covered in a later chapter.

The Jupiter Finger

The length of the Jupiter finger is measured relative to the Saturn finger. Ideally the Jupiter finger should reach about half way up the top phalange of the Saturn finger. A difference of about 5 mm above this point shows a long Jupiter Finger, and a difference of about half an inch below this point shows a short Jupiter Finger. On most people the difference varies by up to 3 mms, which can be disregarded.

The Meaning of the Long or Short Jupiter Finger

If the Jupiter finger is of average length then there is sufficient assertiveness to make one's way in the world.

If the Jupiter Finger is noticeably long, then the assertive powers are very strong. This will show as a strong urge towards leadership, and a need to assert dominance over the environment.

This long Jupiter Finger reveals a strong ego, with very good self-esteem. This 'very good self-esteem' is exaggerated on the very long Jupiter finger, where it reveals arrogance and a sense of superiority.

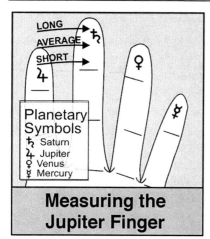

LONG
AVERAGE ♄
SHORT
♃

♀

☿

Planetary
Symbols
♄ Saturn
♃ Jupiter
♀ Venus
☿ Mercury

**Measuring the
Jupiter Finger**

A moderately long Jupiter Finger on the broad muscular hand shows a natural leaning towards management and authority. On the intellectual hand, this feature indicates a sense of superiority regarding intellectual ideas and beliefs.

Where the very long Jupiter Finger shows superiority, the very short Jupiter Finger shows a sense of inferiority. A short Jupiter shows diminished self-esteem and a strong need for praise. The inner world dominates, and the need for outer material reward runs second to the need to be recognised.

Check whether this finger is short on both hands. If for example, a short Jupiter finger is found only on the inner hand, then outer behaviour is motivated by the need for approval and to feel equal to others.

Short Jupiter Fingers on both hands show the need to develop assertive power and pride in oneself. There is a natural tendency is to denigrate self and see others as somehow better or more important. A lot of effort is invested into pleasing others in order to win approval.

Comparing the Jupiter finger to the Venus finger

The Jupiter finger is also measured against the Venus finger. If the Venus finger is considerably longer than the Jupiter finger most of the literature on palmistry says that there is an inferiority complex. However this is only true if the Jupiter finger is actually short. If it is of average length as measured against the Saturn finger and the Venus finger is unusually long, then any lack of confidence is the result of giving inner world directives a higher priority than outer world success. The consequent lack of self esteem in outer world involvement is much more easily corrected than the sense of inferiority indicated by a very short Jupiter finger.

The very short Jupiter finger indicates a much more deeply ingrained sense of inferiority than the low self esteem indicated by the combination of the average length Jupiter finger and the very long Venus finger.

Context

The context indicated by hand shape shows how to interpret long or short Jupiter Fingers. A long Jupiter Finger on the sensitive emotional person's hand (slim, soft and supple) suggests leadership in the caring professions, such as nursing or teaching, or taking the dominant role in the domestic environment.

A short Jupiter Finger on the sensitive emotional person's hand indicates that praise and appreciation is sought when supporting others emotionally, and a willingness to take on more demeaning tasks.

On the intellectual hand (long flat hard with knotty fingers) short Jupiter Fingers show that acceptance is sought through intelligent conversation or persuasion, or by impressing others with clever theories. On this hand shape the short Jupiter Finger often coincides with social withdrawal and escape into the mind.

A long Jupiter finger on the intellectual hand shows a sense of superiority concerning one's belief systems, and a willingness to impose these ideas onto other people. Frequently the intellectual hand shape is found on the hands of sales people. If the Jupiter finger is long and the thumb is also strong then confidence and determination will be defining attributes.

A short Jupiter finger on the broad muscular hand will show Mr. Nice guy or woman, preferring diplomacy over aggression. Socially this shows a pleasant individual seeking social acceptance.

If the Jupiter finger is long on the broad muscular hand then the outgoing nature is backed up by assertiveness, which will suggest leadership, particularly in community groups and organisations.

The Mercury Finger

The length of the Mercury Finger is measured relative to the Venus finger. Again we use half inch rule to show the extremes of long and short.

If the tip of the Mercury Finger reaches the top of the dividing line between the middle and the top sections of the Venus finger (see diagram), then it is considered to be of 'normal' length.

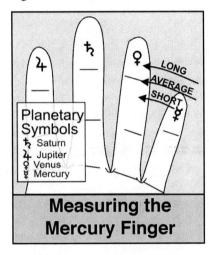

Measuring the Mercury Finger

The Meaning of the Long or Short Mercury Finger

The further the tip of the Mercury Finger passes above this line towards the finger tip, the greater is the ability to communicate. A long Mercury Finger shows someone who is very articulate and has good communication and negotiating skills. When the hands are broad and the thumb is strong these attributes combine to produce good business skills.

The more the tip of the Mercury Finger drops below this line, the greater will be the challenge to communicate. Here there is an internal struggle to communicate the feelings and ideas.

Context

The type of hand on which the Mercury Finger is found will show how to interpret its length. For instance, on the sensitive emotional hand (slim, soft and supple) the basic need is to communicate feelings and to nurture others. On this hand a very long Mercury Finger will indicate that the person speaks a lot about their emotions and their feelings for others.

When this finger is quite short on the sensitive emotional hand these inner feelings cannot be easily expressed, showing a problem that needs to be addressed. In this case the overall hand structure is geared towards the expression of feelings, yet a very short Mercury finger indicates that this need to communicate the inner feelings is frustrated. It is important to direct this person to someone or an organization that can provide corrective training.

On the intellectual's hand (slim, flat, hard with knotty fingers), where the need is to communicate ideas and concepts, a long Mercury Finger enhances the innate ability to communicate ideas, and can bring success in areas such as sales and customer relations.

However a short Mercury Finger on the intellectual's hand is a menace, as it stifles the basic need to express ideas, and shows a tendency for the owner to seek solace in their own inner isolated world. A short Mercury Finger on the intellectual's hand also suggests a frustration in being heard. This individual may talk a lot, but without saying what really matters.

On the broad strong hand a long Mercury Finger usually shows good business skills, and also facilitates community involvement and interaction.

The Venus Finger

The length of the Venus Finger is measured relative to the index finger. Again we use the half inch rule to show extremes of length. Ideally the Venus Finger should reach about half way up the top phalange of the Saturn finger.

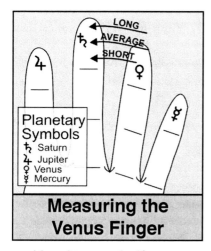

Measuring the Venus Finger

Planetary Symbols
♄ Saturn
♃ Jupiter
♀ Venus
☿ Mercury

The Meaning of the Long or Short Venus Finger

If the Venus and Jupiter Fingers are the same length then there is a balance between the inner and outer worlds. The need for emotional recognition and creativity which is shown by the Venus (ring) Finger is balanced by the assertive drives shown by the Jupiter (index) Finger.

A very long Venus Finger shows that the inner creative forces are very strong. Because this long finger emphasises the inner side of the hand, it shows that the inner world of fantasy and intuition is highly developed. Because the very long Venus finger indicates that the inner world has precedence over the demands of the outer world, ambition and self esteem regarding outer world involvement is diminished. This reading is especially accurate if the Jupiter Finger is also short. Check to see whether the Jupiter Finger is short or recessed into the palm.

Context

Again context is so important. On the broad muscular hand the long Venus Finger shows creative talent which seeks tangible expression. On the intellectual hand this feature indicates belief systems which emphasise non-violence and diplomacy as a means of settling disputes, and creative ideas where the beauty of presentation is important.

A very short Venus Finger shows that the importance of the inner world is diminished, and that the outer world of material success dominates the thinking. On the broad muscular hand the short Venus Finger shows a very practical approach, with little regard for the niceties of presentation. Check whether the Jupiter Finger is very long. Sometimes the Venus Finger can look short, when in fact it is the Jupiter finger which is long.

On the sensitive emotional hand (soft, supple and slender) a very long Venus Finger shows a very intuitive and gentle person, who is driven by the need for appreciation from others. This person will be very responsive and intuitively aware of the emotional needs of family and friends.

The Saturn Finger

The length of the Saturn finger is measured relative to its neighbours, the Jupiter and Venus fingers. We again use the half inch rule for variations in length. However it is rare that the Saturn finger is found to be either long or short. There is little point in doing detailed measurements. Normally your eye will tell you if its length signifies an important deviation from the norm. It will stand out and be noticeable.

The Saturn finger is measured by drawing an imaginary line across the tops of the Jupiter and Venus fingers. If either of these fingers is unusually tall or short just make a 'guess-timate' as to where you think the line should be. This line should pass through the middle of the upper phalange of the Saturn finger. There is no need to be too detailed about this measurement. The measurement is an approximation only. If the middle of this phalange is within 5 mm of this line the Saturn finger is of normal length.

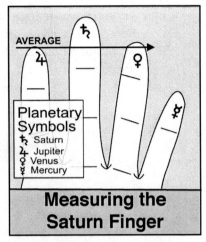

Measuring the Saturn Finger

The Meaning of the Long or Short Saturn Finger

If the Saturn finger stands above its neighbours by approximately half of its upper section (phalange), then there will be a balanced sense of responsibility. The ability to understand what is socially appropriate in terms of responsibility will come naturally. This shows a natural ability to balance the opposing forces of the psyche.

If this finger is excessively long, then the sense of responsibility is over developed. Theoretical and ethical questions receive excessive consideration. How this will be expressed will depend on other factors in the hand.

If this finger is short, then there is a diminished sense of responsibility. Little thought is given to questions of ethics or what is naturally due to others. This is an area about which there is little natural comprehension. This person is often labelled as irresponsible.

Questions to Test Your Understanding
(see Page 154 for answers)

Are the following statements true or false?

1: To assess self esteem the Jupiter finger is measured relative to the Venus finger.

2: A very long Venus finger shows strong self esteem.

3: A very short Saturn finger shows a strong sense of responsibility.

4. A short Mercury Finger on the intellectual's hand shows business acumen.

5. On a soft supple and slender hand a long Venus Finger shows an intuitive and gentle person.

Lesson 14

The Nails

The nails are made of the same materials as the skin and the hair. In hand analysis they are used to assess health and temperament.

Generally the type of finger on which the nail is found determines the shape of the nail. Long fingers have long nails. Short stubby fingers have broad and short nails.

Shape and personality

Just as the colour of the nails should match the colour of the palm, so the shape of the nails should match the shape of the fingers.

Large nails, like large hands, show someone who does not easily get excited. These people do not lose their temper easily.

Large red nails show anger which will be expressed as righteous indignation.

If the nails are pale then anger remains unexpressed and tends to smoulder.

Small nails show excitability.

Long nails show someone who is able to contain their reactions. These people are slow to anger.

Long and narrow nails reveal low energy levels and a reliance on nervous energy.

Short nails show a short temper.

Short and very wide nails show a critical person who often has stomach upsets.

Narrow nails show a more fragile nature in a physical and emotional sense, and a narrow approach to life.

Wide nails show a quick temper, but if the nails are also short the owner does not carry a grudge.

An almond shape is associated with a refined and gentle nature. The length suggests someone slow to anger and the narrowness shows irritability.

A claw shaped nail, where the tip turns inwards, are said to show cruel and mean spirited people. I have not been able to verify this.

Colour and health

Various books encourage the reader to note the colour of the nails. This is only necessary if the colour does not match the colour of the palm.

Blueness shows a health issue and generally indicates reduced hemoglobin. Ask your client to consult a qualified medical practitioner.

Unusually red nails may suggest high blood pressure. They also suggest anger.

Pale nails suggest anaemia.

Yellow spots, brown or greenish nails all suggest medical issues which need to be attended to. Again, encourage your client to consult a qualified medical practitioner.

Other health indications

The following indications, which are sourced from the literature, I have not validated through my own experience. However I encourage those who are interested to investigate this area more fully.

If the nails are bulbous, or have vertical or horizontal ridges or spots, health problems are suggested. Rather than trying to diagnose these problems yourself, encourage your client to consult a qualified medical practitioner.

Very large moons are said to show heart weakness, especially on a conic hand.

Small moons show a longer life and a slower circulation rate.

Very short and very narrow nails are said to show a propensity to heart weakness.

White spots show a lack of calcium and a lack of energy.

Questions to Test Your Understanding (see Page 154 for answers)

Are the following statements true or false?
1: Short nails show a steady temperament.
2: Long nails show the ability to control reactions.
3: Ridges on the nails may show health problems.
4. Almond shaped nails show gentleness and refinement.

Lesson 15

Finger Phalanges — Three Levels of Expression

The two joints on the fingers separate the fingers into three sections, which are called 'phalanges'. The phalanges express the energy of the psyche on three different levels. These three levels follow the same logic as the division of the hands into three areas.

In the case of the overall hand shape, the base of the palm shows the unconscious driving forces within the personality, the upper palm represents the pre-conscious area, and the fingers represent the conscious mind.

Following this same logic, the upper (nail) phalange of the fingers represents higher mental abstract areas, the middle phalange represents the social and business concerns of everyday life, and the lowest phalange represents the physical indulgence of the senses as they relate to the functions of each finger.

The main difference between the hand and the fingers in relation to this threefold division is that the hand symbolises the entire psyche or body/mind, and the fingers represent the application of intelligence on three different levels.

The following chart gives a general overview of how the three different levels of energy can be may be applied to any area or section of the hand. In relation to the fingers this threefold division is applied to the context of each finger's meaning. The upper phalange of each finger describes its application in a mental or theoretical or refined sense, the middle phalange describes its practical application in everyday life, and the lowest phalange shows its basic and most physical expression.

Levels of Meaning Applied to Finger Phalanges

	PSYCHOLOGY	OCCUPATION	ART	ANATOMY
UPPER	CONSCIOUS	MENTAL	ABSTRACT	HEAD
MIDDLE	PRE-CONSCIOUS	SOCIAL PRACTICAL	REALISTIC	THORACIC
LOWER	UNCONSCIOUS	PHYSICAL	EARTHY	ABDOMINAL

The second table provides a brief description of the meaning of each finger phalange.

As a general principle, a narrowing of the phalanges suggests austerity and the application of thought and mental analysis, while a thickening of the phalanges indicates more physical attitudes, sensuality, and if very thick: physical indulgence.

When the middle phalange of the thumb is waisted there is tact. When the thumb is thick and heavy, a heavy and determined attitude to life is indicated.

Again the difference between the left and right hands must be considered. However the size and width of the phalanges are generally the same on both hands.

It is also important to take into account the context of the hand shape - the phalanges must be interpreted within this context.

It is also worth noting that measuring the tip phalange can 'be tricky'. If the finger nails are long then these phalanges appear longer than they really are. If the fingers taper towards the tip then these phalanges may appear shorter than they really are.

Meaning of the Finger Phalanges

	THUMB	JUPITER	SATURN	VENUS	MERCURY
UPPER	ACTION TAKEN APPLIED WILL	IDEALS PRINCIPLES	ETHICS PHILOSOPHY	BEAUTY HARMONY	SCIENCE ELOQUENCE THEORY
MIDDLE	REASONING BEHIND ACTION	AMBITION	CALCULATION MINING AGRICULTURE	DRESS FAME	INDUSTRY BUSINESS COMMONSENSE
LOWER	FEELING BEHIND ACTION	HONOR	MATERIAL GAIN MELANCHOLY SERIOUSNESS	RISK TAKING	SCHEMING HEAVY MUSIC

Questions to Test Your Understanding
(see Page 154 for answers)

Are the following statements true or false?
1: When the thumb is thick and heavy a determined attitude to life is indicated.
2: The phalanges show how the shape of the hand must be interpreted.
3: The middle phalange represents the social and business concerns of everyday life.
4. The phalanges of the fingers represent the application of intelligence on three different levels.
5. A narrowing of the phalanges shows wealth and good living.

Lesson 16

Finger Lean

Terminology

The expression 'finger lean' refers to a sideways bend of the fingers. It does not refer to the very natural curling inwards of the fingers which is seen when something is being gripped or when the hands are partially clenched. The sideways bend of the fingers occurs at the finger joints and is relatively fixed.

Meaning

The fingers represent channels through which the energy of the psyche flows. Each channel corresponds to a personality function. The energy runs from the base of the palm through the hand to the tip of the fingers. When the fingers are straight then there is a free flow of energy indicating that the structure of the personality is sound. When the personality structure is sound there is a greater ability to adjust successfully to life challenges than when some personality function is flawed.

However when a finger is bent sideways then the flow of energy through the finger is also 'bent'. The personality function represented by the bent finger does not function correctly, indicating personality maladjustment.

The general principle of interpretation is that the bent finger will deny the needs represented by the fingers towards which it leans. Sometimes all the fingers lean in a particular direction. More often only one finger is bent. It is also most common for fingers to be bent towards the Saturn finger, and if the Saturn finger is also bent it generally leans towards the Mercury finger.

It is more common to see bent fingers on narrow hands with long fingers. It is less common to see bent fingers on broad hands with short fingers. It is more common to see bent fingers on hands with long fingers than hands with short fingers. One conclusion would be that bent fingers on broad hands with short fingers are more important than bent fingers on hands with longer palms or fingers.

Lean of all the fingers

When all the fingers lean in one direction the personality has a 'lean' or shift towards the part of the personality represented by that part of the hand.

For example, if all the fingers lean towards the outer (thumb) side of the hand, then the needs of others are ignored in order to satisfy inner needs of the ego such as ambition or financial gain. This expression masks some inner hurt (see the lines of the palm), and represents an unconscious strategy to avoid a repeat of that hurt.

A lean of all the fingers towards the inner (little finger) side of the hand shows that personal needs are ignored in order to satisfy the needs of others. This lean towards the inner side of the hand shows an introspective tendency. The inner needs which are ignored may include ambition and financial gain.

Again this represents an adaptation or compensation to avoid a repeat of some hurt. Very often this hurt results from some failure to assert one's needs in the outer world, perhaps some form of humiliation. This feature is often associated with a short index finger (lack of self esteem).

The lean of the Jupiter (index) finger

When the Jupiter finger leans towards the thumb the need to meet the demands of the outer world overwhelms other considerations. One's own success and place in the world dominates the thinking, resulting in a wilful and self centred approach. There will be an obstinate and superior attitude to others, especially if the Jupiter is long.

When the Jupiter finger bends towards the Saturn finger, which is far more common, there is a need to defend oneself against the demands of the outer world. The Jupiter finger will draw upon the negative side of the Saturn finger, producing a strong intellectual and defensive response to any perceived threat. Life will be seen through a set of well organised beliefs that define clearly what is right or wrong, and everyone else's viewpoint will be compared to this structure and disregarded if it does not match up. The capacity for self assertion may be frustrated by a strong sense of guilt and responsibility.

The Jupiter finger can also be understood as the observation finger. It is after all the finger we point with. When it bends towards the middle finger observations are filtered for approval through internalised belief systems, making it very difficult to see what is real and what is not real.

The Saturn (middle) finger

If the Saturn finger is bent towards the thumb (very rare), then the sense of what is right and wrong is biased towards the satisfaction of one's own needs. Other people's needs run a strong second to the satisfaction of one's own pleasures and fantasies. This indicates a self centred approach to life.

When the Saturn finger is bent towards the ring finger, then a sense of guilt and responsibility overwhelms the ability to satisfy one's own needs - personal fulfilment is sacrificed for the purpose of social acceptance. This is a common feature, and shows self-denial in order to please others. This is generally developed as a child when love and acceptance from one's parents was experienced as being conditional upon doing what they wanted. Please mum and dad, and be loved. Fail to please mum and dad and there will be no love.

From the child's perspective there is no choice. The greater the bend, the greater is the tendency to deny one's own needs to please others. Recent studies on co-dependence have clarified many of the behavioural dynamics associated with this feature. If you are consulting people it is highly recommended that you study the subject and solutions that are offered.

The key words for the inward bend of the middle finger are 'co-dependence' and 'guilt'. The guilt arises when one ignores the demands of the 'inner parents', and satisfies one's own needs. This is often labelled as 'selfish'.

The Venus (ring) finger

When the Venus finger leans towards the Saturn finger the sense of responsibility is amplified, showing a difficulty in enjoying pleasure for its own sake.

In this case pleasure often comes from seeing other people have pleasure (vicarious pleasure). There is a strong drive to encourage others to have fun. Although vicarious pleasure is better than none at all, the personality remains somewhat out of focus in terms of genuine fulfilment.

When the ring finger bends towards the little finger, then the hand takes on an unusual physical appearance expression reminiscent of some science fiction gesture of salute. This indicates a preoccupation with inner fantasies which creates a separation from others, and is often the sign of the loner or eccentric. Emotional fulfilment may be sought outside the norms of society. The presence of this feature on both hands indicates a unique and perhaps anti-social individual.

The Mercury (little) finger

A lean of the Mercury finger towards the ring finger reveals that the ability to communicate the inner needs has been cramped at an early age, and circuitous methods are used to communicate wants and desires. A curved Mercury finger shows a roundabout (curved) method of self-expression. There is a difficulty with direct communication.

From a childhood developmental perspective, this feature often suggests an expectation that the parents would disapprove of direct demands, and new (sometimes sneaky) communication methods are invented. Consequently there is a difficulty in adult years in openly expressing true feelings, because of some fear of rejection or hurt.

Should the Mercury finger lean away from the Venus finger (very rare), communication may be very unique or anti-social. This may have consequences in sexual expression.

Questions to Test Your Understanding
(see Page 154 for answers)

Are the following statements true or false?

1: When a finger is bent sideways then the flow of energy through the finger is hindered.

2: The Jupiter finger leaning towards the Saturn Finger shows communication problems.

3: When the Saturn finger bends towards the Venus finger, guilt and responsibility are strong forces within the psyche.

4. A lean of all the fingers towards Mercury shows the urge to satisfy the needs of others.

Lesson 17

The Thumb

The thumb is a most distinctive human feature. It links the unconscious world to the conscious will. This association with the will indicates that there is a clear correlation with the planet Mars as described in astrology. The thumb describes how the personal will is applied. The information below provides this description.

The 3 sections

There are 3 sections to the thumb: the tip, the middle section, and the ball of the thumb (the Sun Mount).

The tip of the thumb shows how we act, the middle section shows how much reasoning is behind our actions, and the size of the Sun Mount shows how much this reasoning is backed up by warmth and enthusiasm.

Measuring strength

The strength of the thumb is shown by a combination of length, rigidity and thickness – these will be described in a later lesson.

The strong thumb represents willpower backed by reason and the determination to act. It represents forceful willpower, and the ability to resist temptation. People with strong thumbs are directed by reason.

By contrast, a weak or small thumb shows that there is insufficient willpower to resist temptation. This person is at the mercy of their desires and emotions and is led by the heart.

Consequently those with large or strong thumbs provide leadership, while those with weak thumbs follow.

High and Low set thumbs

The two subjects in Picasa Album Hands Oct 09 have high set thumbs. High set thumbs show less adaptability than low set thumbs, and a greater emphasis is placed on logic and reason.

By contrast low set thumbs are associated with a more instinctive response to life's challenges and opportunities. Low set thumb people are generally more responsive to others in an emotional sense and less restrained by mental attitudes. To assess whether a thumb is high or low set by ask the subject to open the thumb out as far as it will go.

Measuring the Thumb

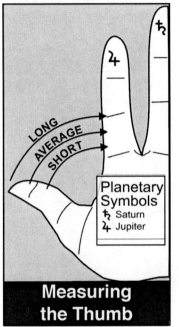

Measuring the Thumb

The length of the thumb is measured by laying it flat against the Jupiter Finger. The hand should be flat with the fingers and palm aligned in a straight line when viewed sideways. The thumb should be relaxed.

Again we use the 5 mm rule to show extremes of length. Ideally the thumb should reach about half way up the lower phalange of the Jupiter Finger.

However in this case it is not only its length which needs to be measured, but also its suppleness, its thickness and width on the nail and middle phalanges, and whether it is set high or low. Suppleness (flexibility) diminishes strength, but a thumb which is too stiff will show rigidity of the personality and a rigid approach to life.

The Meaning of the Long or Short Thumb

A strong or long thumb represents forceful willpower, and the ability to overcome obstacles and resist temptation. By contrast, a weak or small thumb shows that there is insufficient willpower to overcome obstacles or resist temptation. This person is at the mercy of their desires and emotions.

Questions to Test Your Understanding
(see Page 154 for answers)

Are the following statements true or false?
1: Low set thumbs reveal an instinctive approach to life.
2: The thumb is measured by the length of the Saturn Finger.
3: A strong thumb shows willpower.
4. A lean of all the fingers towards Mercury shows the urge to satisfy the needs of others.

Section 3
The Lines

Lesson 18

The Lines of the Palm

General characteristics

The lines of the palm are like channels of energy, linking one area of the palm to another. A useful analogy is to think of them as rivers. Thus a deep red line, like a deep fast flowing river, shows strong vital energies. A broad shallow line, like a broad shallow river, shows sluggish energy.

In the following lessons the meaning of each of the main lines will be discussed separately.

Branches

Branches from lines show diversions of energy. The meaning of a branch is derived from the type of energy represented by the area on which it terminates.

Context

Strong hands should contain strong lines, and weak hands should contain weak lines. A weak hand with strong lines indicates that the energy supply will soon become exhausted. A strong hand with weak lines suggests that the underlying energy has no outlet, resulting in tension and unfulfilled desires.

There are 3 types of lines:

1. The main lines (Life, Head, Heart, and Saturn Lines);
2. The secondary lines. These are less important; and
3. Tertiary lines, which include all the threadlike minor lines. These lines are generally an expression of nervous energy.

The main lines provide the 'main' story. Their general characteristics when combined with the type of hand on which they are found give you 'the big picture' of a person's life. When understood within the context of the hands on which they are found, they show the basic psychological make-up.

The secondary lines are secondary to the main story. While each has its own definite meaning, its interpretation must include the 'big picture' shown by the major lines and the overall hand shape. A more 'major' secondary line, included by some authors in the category of the main lines, is the Mercury Line, which runs from the lower palm towards the Mercury finger.

The tertiary lines are of less importance individually. However an assessment of their overall number and which area of the palm they occupy provides valuable information concerning stress and nervous energy. On some hand types, such as the sensitive emotional hand, some tertiary lines are a natural feature. On other hands, such as the elementary earth hand, they indicate a problem.

Primary Lines

The three primary lines are the Life Line, the Head Line and the Heart Line. Except in cases where the Heart and Head Lines are fused together, these 3 lines are found on almost all palms.

Like the primary hand types, these 3 lines correspond to major human functions: thinking, feeling and physical action (doing). They also correspond to 3 important organs of the body: the heart (Heart Line), the brain (the Head Line), and the spine (the Life Line).

The Life Line is the most important line on the earth hand, because it specifically relates to physical vitality, which is so important to the person with this hand. This is the line of vitality - the channel through which the life force flows. Its very presence shows the capacity for physical life. Everybody alive has a Life Line or at least a portion of a Life Line.

The condition of this line is the primary indicator of physical health, even though there is another line on the palm called The Health Line. There is some similarity with astrology here in that the first house of the horoscope represents the physical vitality and the sixth house represents illness. Defects on the Life Line (such as islands, breaks, bars, or a fading of the line) always show a significant health problem.

The Head Line shows the style of thinking, for example, whether it is imaginative or logical, the clarity and application of thought. The strength of this line is very important for the person with The Philosophical Hand, because ideas and thinking are so important to this person. Defects on this line show either mental trauma, or problems with the brain.

The Heart Line records to the feelings - how the person feels within themselves and how they feel towards other people. This line also shows the style of emotional expression -whether, for example, the person responds to physical affection or mental stimulation (romance). The condition of this line is very important for the person with the Sensitive Emotional Hand, because the expression of love and emotion is vital to their happiness.

The Combination Line is the Head Line and the Heart Line fused into one line, and is found on about 5% of the population, spread through different personality types, although in greater concentration on earth hands. The Combination Line shows that the feelings and thoughts run through the same channel, which gives great power of concentration when thoughts and feelings are aligned, alternating with periods of confusion when the thoughts and feelings are not aligned.

The Saturn Line shows how the inner feelings find fulfilment in the outer world of material reality. This line is frequently called the 'Fate Line' which has the unfortunate connotation of pre-destiny and inevitability. It reveals the satisfaction with the material world as well as social integration.

Hand Types and Primary Line Correspondence

On the hand which shows that the dominant experience of life is physical and practical, a strong Life Line is vital to happiness. These hands are broad large and muscular with medium to coarse skin texture. Weaknesses of the Life Line on this hand type indicate a diminished capacity to experience and enjoy the physical world. Yes a strong Life Line is important for any hand, but is vitally important on the physical/practical hand.

The most important line on the thinker's hand is the Head Line. The thinker's hand generally has well defined knuckles on the fingers, and a long and hard flat palm. If the Head Line on this hand has defects (islands, breaks or fading), then the owner's major asset is diminished.

On the sensitive emotional hand the most important line is the Heart Line. The sensitive emotional hand is soft slender and supple. Malfunctioning of this line on the sensitive emotional hand shows that the owner's life is compromised.

Secondary Lines

The secondary lines record the development and further refinement of the main lines. Their presence elevates the hand structure beyond the elementary type showing a higher development of the cerebral nervous system.

These will be discussed in the chapter following a discussion of the main lines.

The Overall Appearance of the Lines

While it is important to analyse each line separately, the overall appearance of the lines reveals the mental/emotional state of health. For example, if the overall picture shows that the lines are clear and distinct and continuous then the person is clear and direct and able to maintain focus. However if the lines are all broken up then the person is 'all broken up' in some sense. If the lines look like an absolute mess and are confusing to read then we can say that the person is in a mess and confused.

The ability to assess the overall appearance comes with experience and is difficult to teach. It is worthwhile noting your impression of each set of hands as they are presented. The ability to do this is more intuitive than logical and is worthwhile practising at every opportunity. It is best to go with your first impression without too much deliberation. You will improve with practise.

5 Basic Rules to Follow When Interpreting the Lines of the Palm

1. Examine the overall hand structure on which the lines to establish what type of needs the person is trying to fulfil through the lines. The hand structure includes the palm width, overall finger length, individual finger length, hardness, skin texture, flexibility, fingerprints, thumb size and setting, and finger tips. How well do the lines give expression to this structure?

2. The thick end of a line represents its beginning, and the thinnest end represents its end.

3. Check which areas of the palm the line links together. This meaning must be read according to the hand structure. To understand what areas are being linked together, it is necessary to understand the zones of the palm. The lines are like channels of energy linking one area of the palm to another.

4. The areas towards which branches from a line go show what expression the meaning of the line takes. Thus, for example, a major branch from the head line to the Venus zone shows thinking about art - art and style and perhaps creativity are the focus of the mind.

5. The quality of a line must also be taken into account...its depth, colour, width, islands, cross lines, fraying, dots, and general appearance. These factors reveal the character of the energy flow, and hence the character of its expression.

How to Interpret the Appearance of a Line

The descriptions below apply to the lines in general as well as to particular lines.

Clear even lines: Show that the energy of the line is channelled evenly and directly. This reflects that the function of the line is accomplished well. This is healthy if there are not too many lines.

Deep lines: Show a strong energy flow. If you think of the lines as rivers of energy you will easily appreciate their meaning. Expect deep lines on a strong thick hand. On a thin fragile looking hand they indicate a tendency to burn out.

Shallow broad lines: Show comparative weakness, discouragement, and a sluggish approach to life. To achieve results the owner needs to expend great effort, which is only possible if the thumb is strong.

Uneven lines: Shows a spasmodic transmission of energy. The qualities represented by the line will wax and wane. The intensity of the energy will vary. Greater depth shows greater intensity. Thinning shows a weakening of resolve to express the quality represented by the line.

A split line: Shows a diversion of energy into two or more areas. The character of the line will be altered by the meaning of the zone on which the split line terminates. When the split travels only a short distance the split will be less important than those which travel a large distance. **Tasselled termination:** This is similar to a split with the difference that this line splits into

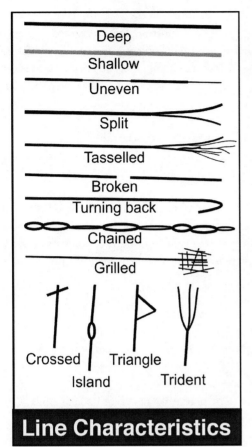

Deep

Shallow

Uneven

Split

Tasselled

Broken

Turning back

Chained

Grilled

Crossed   Triangle

Island   Trident

Line Characteristics

many fine strands and fades out. This shows that the energy of the line is scattered and diffused at this point. This has the effect of weakening the overall character of the line.

Broken line: Indicate a break in the energy flow. Small breaks are less serious than large breaks. The wider the space between the broken ends the more serious is the problem. At the time of the break the quality of the line cannot be expressed. Thus a break in the vitality line shows little vitality. A break in the heart line shows heartbreak. The negative effect of breaks are minimised and repaired by overlapping lines, a sister line running alongside the break, or by a square formed around the break.

A line turning back on its source: Shows a serious defect in the functioning of the line. This sign is fortunately very rare. The energy of this line is turned back towards its source showing internal frustration.

Chained line: This line has the appearance of a series of islands which are joined together for a certain distance or the entire length. This represents a continuous series of obstructions to the free flow of energy. If the chaining is considerable it can only be repaired by a sister line.

A grilled line: This is indicated by a criss-crossing of the line by vertical or horizontal lines. The energy of the line is dissipated by the intersecting lines. The area over which the grille is placed is influenced in a negative way. This is more serious if the intersecting lines are heavy and numerous. Grilles often suggest a health defect.

Crossed line: This is more serious than a grille because there is no assistance from other lines. Crossed lines always indicate a major challenge to be overcome.

A line intersected by a cross: Represents a serious challenge to be overcome.

A line containing an island: Always indicate an obstacle impeding the free flow of energy through the line. An islanded line splits and then rejoins itself. The island weakens the strength and force of the line by dividing it temporarily into two branches, each of half strength. Islands generally indicate an emotional problem especially on the Heart Line. On the Head Line they indicate emotional disturbance affecting the mind. This needs to be a time of healing.

A line with a triangle upon it: Whether formed by two small branches rising to meet at a point, or a complete triangle placed over the line, a triangle a traditionally interpreted as a very beneficial sign. The area of the hand over which it is placed will indicates the quality which is emphasised. For example over the area beneath the little finger it suggests the gift of persuasion and business acumen. Under the middle finger it suggests scholastic research or intellectual achievement if found on an intellectual hand.

A trident at the upper end of a line: Seen as a mark of great success according to the meaning of the line on which it is found. This interpretation must be backed up by other indications such as a strong thumb, and interpreted according to the type of hand on which it is found.

Few lines: Show enjoyment of earthy simplicity with a preference for an outdoor or country lifestyle. On narrow palms the avenues available to express feelings and thoughts are fewer in number. On narrow hard palms with knuckled fingers strong beliefs are held about a smaller number of interests. On slender soft and supple hands the emotions are focused into a small number of areas.

Numerous lines : An active mind and well developed nervous system.

On narrow palms numerous lines show that the ability to express the internal world is assisted by mental development and refinement.

On broad palms numerous lines indicate a diversity of practical talents and social skills. On narrow hard hands numerous lines emphasis intellectual development.

On soft slender hands it is normal to find numerous lines. Few lines on this hand type would indicate someone who leads a simpler life, often living in a rural setting, with fewer concerns to tax the mind and nervous system.

Numerous broken lines indicate anxiety, stress and possible neurosis.

Long deep clear lines show sustained vitality and enthusiasm for the meaning represented by the line.

Very red lines indicate passion and a fiery temperament.

Deep red lines on a weak fragile hand indicate a tendency to burn out.

Fine wispy and weak lines on a powerful thick hand show A tendency to overload and explode with frustrated energy.

Questions to Test Your Understanding
(see Page 154 for answers)

Are the following statements true or false?

1: Broken lines show a disruption of the energy flow represented by the line.

2: When the overall appearance of the lines looks confused nutritional supplements are required.

3: Islands on a main line always indicate a problem with the function represented by that line.

4. If the overall line structure looks clear and direct neurosis is present.

5. A line structure that looks busy but clear shows a busy mind that is functioning well.

Lesson 19

The Life Line

The Life Line is the first line that should be examined when reading the hands. It provides a recording of the strength of the life force which empowers every other human faculty. No matter what wonderful assets are revealed elsewhere in the hands, if the Life Line is weak or faulty then the promise of these assets cannot be completely fulfilled.

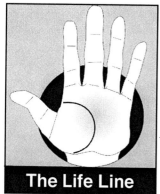

The Life Line

The Life Line shows how well the physical mental and emotional expressions are energised. When the Life Line is weak the individual is thrown upon the resources of their nervous system and is weakened. In this situation every function is stressed and strained and problems are likely to manifest in the area that is weakest. The area that is weakest might be shown within the structure of the hand such as in unusual finger length, or within the process of this structure in the other main lines: Heart, Head or Saturn. Your judgement will also be informed by the overall appearance of the lines on the palm.

There is always a Life Line on the palms; even it is only very short and weak. Every living person possesses a Life Line on each hand. The Life Line reveals the capacity for physical existence.

For those with astrological knowledge, the Life Line can be compared to the first house and its ruler. It is to the first house and its ruler that we look to ascertain the individual's vitality. Likewise in palmistry the Life Line reveals the health and vitality of the individual.

The life line expresses the energy stored in the Sun Mount, the mount of vitality. When this mount is firm and full there are strong passionate energies seeking expression. Here a strong and clear Life Line reveals the capacity to give fulfilment to the vital energies of vim and vigour, passion and enthusiasm.

The Life Line may begin from two directions. Reading from the beginning above the thumb and under the index finger, is the most well understood method. Here it is read downwards towards the wrist. This method shows the capacity for physical survival in the outside world. This line records basic physical health and well being. Its quality also reflects the family home.

The Life Line is an excellent indicator of health, especially when its features are matched with those of the other main lines. Breaks in the other main lines can be assessed and validated for their importance by studying the corresponding age on the Life Line.

The Life Line records the physical health and vitality. It is the most important line on the hand in regard to health. The strength of the Life Line shows vim and vigour, "get-up-and-go", enthusiasm, passion and drive.

The Life Line links the lowest area of the palm, which represents the most instinctive and visceral part of the psyche, to the outer world. This connection reveals the meaning of the Life Line – how the inner physical drives are fulfilled in the outer physical world.

The Life Line is like the engine of the personality, particularly in regard to the physical constitution.

Engine Size

The Life Line encircles the padded mount at the base of the thumb, and draws its energy from this area. If this padded mount is high and thick, then the Life Line has a plentiful supply of energy to draw upon. A deep well marked Life Line records physical dynamism, strong vitality and enthusiasm for a vigorous lifestyle.

When the Life Line moves out across the palm in a wide arc, then the Mount of the Sun is large and the energies contained within it are well developed. In this case there is great scope for warmth and affection; love, understanding and passion. This indicates an outgoing social person. If the skin texture is coarse, the combination shows a preference for outdoors activity. If the skin texture is fine then skill and finesse will be added to physical activity, and a profession using mental skills will be preferred.

It is more common and more natural to find a broad sweeping Life Line on a broad palm. On a narrow palm such a widely arced Life Line would indicate someone at odds with themselves - an outgoing personality with less capacity to maintain the vigorous and social lifestyle they desire.

However if the Life Line stays close to the thumb, and makes only a narrow arc across the palm, then the size of the Mount of the Sun is diminished, and so are the qualities associated with it. This person is colder, more reserved and introspective than the person with the widely arced Life Line. An indoors lifestyle is preferred. This Life Line is more suited to the narrow palm.

Flat Battery

When the padded area at the base of the thumb (Sun Mount) is flat and soft, then there is little energy to draw upon. In this case a strong Life Line is unable to express the same vitality and enthusiasm as the one in the previous example – there will be less stamina and a tendency to burn out more quickly. A weaker Life Line here, which normally looks finer or thinner, reflects a lower level of physical energy, with little enthusiasm for physical exertion.

Breaks, islands, dots and fraying of the Life Line all record ill health, lowered vitality and enthusiasm for physical exertion at the time when they occur.

Worry Lines
crossing the Life Line

Worry Lines

Lines crossing the Life Line and going out into the palm indicate drainage of physical energy. This energy drain is normally associated with worry and anxiety. These are frequently called worry lines by traditional palmists. On the physical level they are associated with a loss of vitamins and minerals, which is frequently accompanied by stress.

On the social level numerous fine lines crossing the Life Line are associated with interference of other people – "giving one's power away". Indian palmists often associate these lines with particular people. Assess the length of the index finger for self assertive skills, an inward bend of the middle finger for self sacrifice, and the thumb for determination. It may be that the person simply needs to learn how to say "NO".

The Life Line is also associated with family life, particularly in Chinese palmistry. Thus a strong clear unbroken Life Line is an indicator of a stable home life, particularly when it curls back in under the base of the thumb. A Life Line that is broken in many places shows instability at home, as well as ill health.

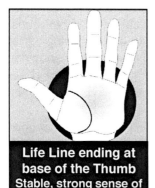

Life Line ending at
base of the Thumb
Stable, strong sense of
roots, home and family

The Stable Life Line

A Life Line which is continuous and curls back in under the base of the thumb shows a strong sense of home and family – 'a sense of roots'. This line often shows a strong attachment to the original home, or property – frequently to the land.

When a stable Life Line formation is found on both hands this interpretation is more certain.

The Wanderer's Life Line

A Life Line which crosses the Mount of the Moon indicates a restless yearning for 'greener pastures'. This is the hand of the person who loves to travel and explore distant and exotic places. This shows a restless and unstable personality – unstable in the sense that there is a constant wish to 'move on'.

The Mount of the Moon is the area of instincts, and a Life Line ending on this mount indicates that the personality is driven by instincts which are unexplained. Nervousness is also shown by this type of Life Line.

Life Line ending on Mount of the Moon Restless Traveler

If the Wanderer's Life Line is found on the passive hand, and the Stable Life Line is found on the active hand, then there is a strong urge to travel and explore, and the contrary wish to come home. This indicates a life of restriction, where the inner need to roam is frustrated.

When the reverse is true, with the Stable Life Line found on the passive hand and the Wanderer's Life Line on the active hand, then the person is most likely to roam and travel, but is also likely to return home. This is the person who wants to travel but also gets homesick. This person may also find travel exhausting.

Sometimes the lower end of the Life Line is found between these two extremes near the centre of the wrist. This indicates a certain vagueness and uncertainty about the personality. It shows restlessness, is similar to the Wanderer's Life Line, but to a lesser extent.

The length of the Life Line

At this point I would like to dispel some inaccurate myths about the Life Line: A long Life Line shows that qualities of endurance and stamina improve the chances of a long life. However a long Life Line by no means guarantees a long life and other factors may have to be assessed.

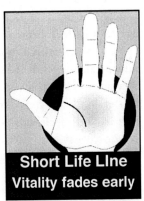

Short Life LIne Vitality fades early

A short Life Line:

This person will be restricted to living mainly on nervous energy at the time when the Life Line ceases. However death is by no means certain as many of the uneducated tend to believe. It is of less importance if it is found only on one hand. It does however indicate serious weakness at its ending point. Precautionary measures will need to be taken well before that time.

Interpreting the beginning of the Life Line

The Life Line is normally interpreted as beginning from the upper palm. Following the logic that says lines are energised through the base of the palm from the wrist and that this energy flow through the hand is expressed through the finger tips, we may also read the Life Line upwards from the wrist. This reading provides a sense of how the early psychological needs for love and nurture find fulfilment in the outer world.

In these lessons we shall restrict our interpretation to the Life Line as read downwards away from the wrist.

See the illustrations on the next page.

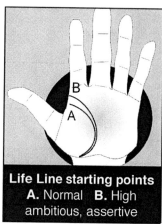

Life Line starting points
A. Normal   **B.** High
ambitious, assertive

Beginning (A)

This is the 'normal' beginning of the line and shows balance between ambition and aggression, achievement and defensiveness. This is by far the most common source of the Life Line.

High beginning (B)

This beginning point activates the Jupiter zone and extends the boundary of the Outer Mars Mount. The extension of the Outer Mars Mount increases aggressive drives. It is important to direct these assertive drives into something naturally competitive yet relatively harmless such as sports and martial arts.

The beginning of the Life Line on the Jupiter Zone indicates ambition to achieve worldly position. A strong thumb here will be of great assistance in directing these powerful drives.

The higher up on the Jupiter Zone the Life Line beginning point is placed the more ambition and assertiveness is indicated.

Beginning tied to the Head Line

When the upper end of the Life Line is joined to the Head Line, then a cautious attitude is present. The degree of caution and dependence is indicated by the length of the join – the longer the join the more cautious and dependent is the personality.

The further along the Head Line it is joined, the more caution and dependence is indicated. This person thinks before they act – physical action (the Life Line) is taken only after the matter has been considered mentally (the Head Line). Caution in both decision making and self expression colours this person's behaviour. The longer the join, the more timid is the

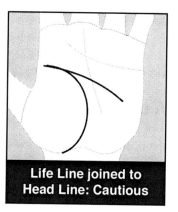

Life Line joined to
Head Line: Cautious

outlook. This beginning is more common on broad palms than on narrow palms.

Beginning separated from the Head Line

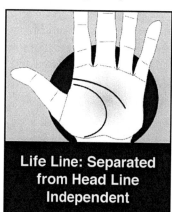

Life Line: Separated
from Head Line
Independent

When the upper end of the Life Line is separate to the Head Line then independence is indicated. The bigger the gap between the Head Line and the Life Line, the greater is the indication of independence. This also indicates that the person is headstrong – tends to rush in without thinking.

Feelings of independence and a tendency to do or say things without thinking becomes more pronounced the wider the gap between the Life Line and the Head Line. This tendency to act rashly is sometimes humorously called "foot-in-mouth-disease". This feature is more common on soft slender hands.

Interpreting the end of the Life Line

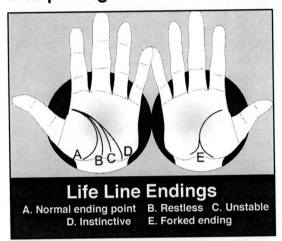

Life Line Endings
A. Normal ending point B. Restless C. Unstable
D. Instinctive E. Forked ending

Ending at A: This indicates feelings of stability and a strong affinity with the land, home and family. This ending is common on earth hands. It adds strength on weaker hands.

Ending at B: This ending at the centre of the wrist shows less stability and less sense of belonging. The area at the centre of the wrist is the seat of emotion, receptivity and the primary 'birth zone'. It is often associated with water, and lifestyles associated with water. This ending suggests emotional instability and over sensitivity.

Ending at C: This ending is upon the Mount of the Moon (mystery and imagination). It shows instability and restlessness. It is often called 'the travel line'. It does indicate a restless spirit whose challenge is in finding a stable connection with others. Because the Life Line can also be read from the wrist upwards to indicate psychological development, this ending suggests a difficulty in bonding in childhood. The result is an unstable base for the emotions.

Ending at D: This ending deep in the base of the Mount of the moon taps into the collective unconscious, indicating deep instinctual driving forces beyond the realm of the consciousness ego. This ending suggests compulsive and obsessive drives which may push the limits of mortality.

Ending at E: A forked ending shows a desire to travel and a desire to stay home. This will sometimes indicate someone who has 2 places of residence, one being in a distant country or location. More often it shows frequent travel but having a stable place of residence.

Ending with a tasselled or frayed appearance where the line splits into fine branches: This represents ill-health in old age and deterioration in health.

Interpreting branches from the Life Line

Lines from the Life Line energise and excite the quality of the zone on which they terminate. They overall shape of the hands will provide guidelines as to how this energy will be expressed. Also look at the quality of the Life Line to assess the quality of energy being transmitted.

The energy diversion is a two way process, with the quality of the zone on which the branch terminates adding to the quality of the Life Line.

Branch A shows that the Jupiter Zone is excited, resulting in ambitious aspirations.

ENERGY & ENTHUSIASM FOR
A. Ambitious projects, leadership
B. Study, career, organization
C. Art, creativity and beauty
D. Business, communication, sales
E. Travel, faraway places, mystery, imagination, mystical experiences

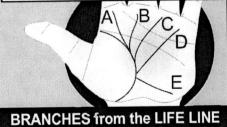

BRANCHES from the LIFE LINE

The longest section of the Jupiter finger will suggest the area of intended achievement.

Branch B shows that vitality is added to material gain, as well as to thoughtful, organisational and studious pursuits. If the middle finger section is the longest, then business and social concerns will be the area of focus.

This line also functions as a Saturn Line (often called the 'Fate Line' in the literature). The Saturn Line is treated separately in these lessons as a major line.

Branch C indicates that vitality and enthusiasm are directed towards artistry and talented self expression. If the lowest finger section is the longest, then ostentatious display is indicated.

Branch D shows that vitality energises the Mercurial qualities of exchange and communication. Here the overall shape of the hand will indicate the type of energy seeking expression.

For example on a coarse thick hand a branch from the Life Line to the Mercury Zone suggests industry and money making for its own sake. On a hand showing intellect and verbal skills this line amplifies the communication and presentation skills.

This branch is usually called 'The Mercury Line' and is treated separately in this book under the classification of secondary lines.

Dating the Life Line:

Of the several different dating systems described in the books I have found the one described below to be the most accurate.

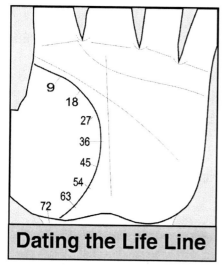

Dating the Life Line

This method dates the life up until 72 years of age. While it is now very common for people to live up until 80 - 90 years of age, this system works very effectively for people under 72 years of age.

The Life is divided in half with the halfway point indicating 36 years of age. The remaining sections of the Life Line are then sub-divided proportionately. Because the Life Line is curved it is necessary to do a 'guess-timate'.

It must be remembered that the lines can and do often change, and the Life Line can grow, gaps in the Life Line can be repaired, and a frayed ending of the Life Line can grow into a stronger formation if preventative health measures are taken.

Anatomy

On an anatomical level the Life Line reflects the nervous condition of the spine. The top of the Life Line (nearest the Jupiter finger) represents the neck and the lower end of the Life Line reflects the coccyx. Breaks or defects in the Life Line often reflect a weakness in the associated part of the spine. Such breaks or defects may also reflect illness at the time indicated by the break in the Life Line (see dating above) as well as changes in lifestyle at the same time. Because the Life Line has an association with family, these changes may also reflect changes in family structure.

Questions to Test Your Understanding
(see Page 155 for answers)

Are the following statements true or false?

1: When the Life Line is linked to the Head Line it shows that action is guided by thought.
2: When the Life Line ends on the Mount of the Moon there is restlessness and a desire for travel.
3: Breaks in the Life Line show holidays.
4. A short Life Line always shows a short life.
5. The Life Line that is deep and red shows vitality enthusiasm and passion.

Lesson 20

The Head Line

General meaning

The lower transverse line of the palm is called "The Head Line". This line records the scope and application of intelligence. The Head Line is a measure of mental expression and also records emotional and other influences. This line records the style of thinking. The type of intelligence being recorded is shown by the shape of the hand. The Head Line has been called "the compass of the hand" by Noel Jaquin as it shows the direction to which thought is applied.

In "Secrets of Hand Reading" Noel Jaquin says: "This important line betrays the scope of the mind, its scope indicates the scope in which the mind can operate efficiently and with complete understanding".

As with all the lines, the Head Line only shows the thought process relating to the personality type as revealed by the overall hand structure. The shape of the finger tips shows the style of expression, and the finger prints show the genetic patterns relating to this expression. The capacity to concentrate is shown by the thumb, and the capacity to communicate this intelligence is shown by the little finger.

Beginning points

The Head Line has its natural beginning in the lower Jupiter zone, near to or touching the Life Line. Its natural termination is on the percussion of the hand, usually ending between the Venus and Mercury fingers.

If the Head Line begins from the Jupiter finger or high on the Jupiter mount then there is a powerful sense of pride, leadership capacity, impulsive self expression, and a strong sense of social worth combined with a good sense of humour. If the Jupiter finger is of at least average length then this person will express themselves with great confidence.

If the Head Line begins from lower on the Jupiter zone then these qualities are moderated. There is an ease in handling others and a natural sense of authority, a good sense of humour and impulsiveness. On a thick earthy hand these qualities will be expressed in a clumsy manner. On a hand which shows a preference for refinement and intellectual expression these qualities will be channelled into refined theoretical expression and intellectual persuasion. On a soft and supple hand which indicates a rich emotional life these confident and impulsive attitudes will find expression in caring for others, either in the family or community.

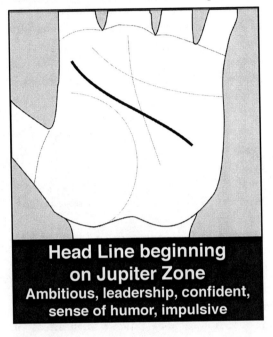

Head Line beginning on Jupiter Zone
Ambitious, leadership, confident, sense of humor, impulsive

As mentioned in Lesson 18: the Life Line, if the Head Line is linked with the Life Line it indicates caution, the degree of which depends on the length of its connection to the Life Line.

If the Head Line begins inside the Life Line on the Mount of Outer Mars, there will be a defensive and uncertain approach to life, intense, changeable and sometimes aggressive.

Anatomical correspondence

On an anatomical level this line reflects the brain. Breaks or disturbances on the Head Line may indicate disturbances to the physical brain.

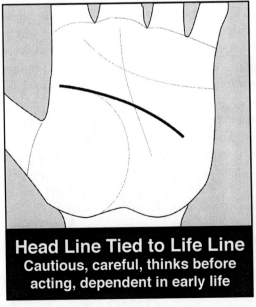

Head Line Tied to Life Line
Cautious, careful, thinks before acting, dependent in early life

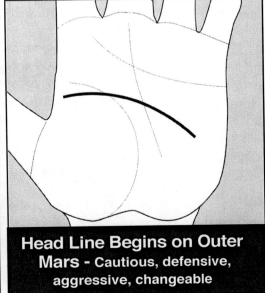

Head Line Begins on Outer Mars - Cautious, defensive, aggressive, changeable

The straight Head Line: The logical thinker

The greater the straightness of the Head Line across the hand, the more that person is able to calculate, is logical and businesslike. The very straight Head Line has no time for nebulous theories. This type of Head Line is more common on broad palms. The straighter the Head Line runs

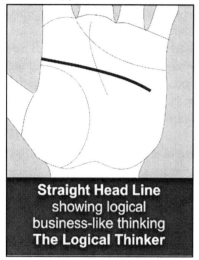

Straight Head Line showing logical business-like thinking The Logical Thinker

across the hand, the greater is the logical capacity. A very straight Head Line shows the ability to calculate and plan ahead. it shows "a straight and level headed" approach to life. The owner of this Head Line appreciates the practical and material aspects of life. When a straight Head Line is combined with a strong thumb, it shows the ability to stay in control of the feelings, and also the wish to be in control.

The Head Line which extends to the zone of Inner Mars, which is located just above the Mount of the Moon, inner resolve and forceful attitudes are more apparent. If the hand shape reveals strong physical inclinations, then competitive sports, management and military pursuits may appeal.

A very straight and undifferentiated line indicates an intellect that is rigid within itself, allowing no outside influence to impact upon the flow of thought. If such a straight undifferentiated line is found upon a stiff rigid hand then it reveals a very self absorbed person with no regard for the opinion of others but only for their own material welfare, with little or no ability to share feelings with others.

However if this line contains indications of feeling responses, such a small defects or branches, then they can be touched by the needs of others and have a greater capacity to share in an emotional and intellectual sense.

Downward curve: The imaginative person

The greater the downward curve of the Head Line towards the Mount of the Moon, the more the imagination takes hold. A steep downward curve terminating on the Mount of the Moon indicates a mind capable of much fantasy. This shows a very intuitive person with a rich imagi-

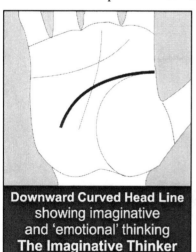

Downward Curved Head Line showing imaginative and 'emotional' thinking The Imaginative Thinker

nation. With square fingertips this person may be very good at design. This type of Head Line is most common on sensitive emotional hands, which are slender soft and supple.

The downward curve adds imagination and dramatic emotional style to the thinking process, as well as a more relaxed expression than is found on the straight Head Line. The thinking is more superstitious and less methodical than the straight Head Line. This line is frequently associated with artistic expression in the old books. However it only shows artistic talent if it is accompanied by a large Mount of the Moon, or a Venus Line, or a long ring finger. The owner of the downward curving Head Line can visualise possibilities, and is more inclined to creative expression, poetry and romance.

Steep Downward curve: The creative dreamer

When the Head Line drops very low into the palm, the imaginative qualities are strongly emphasised. This is the hand of the very emotional person, who experiences the highs and lows of life. If the hand is soft and flexible, then there is little emotional restraint, and depression and suicidal tendencies are possible, especially if the thumb is also weak or short.

On a broad strong well padded palm, this steeply curving Head Line shows a very creative person who seeks a practical outlet, but with a tendency to go to extremes. On any hand type this line indicates a very vivid imagination, especially if it is found on both hands. Because of its extra length, this Lunar Head Line offers great scope for intellectual achievements, but only on a hand which has strength, such as a strong thumb and firmness. On a weak hand this long and deep curving Head Line reveals little capacity to control the extremes of thinking, often resulting in serious depression, craziness, and sometimes suicide.

Gentle curve: The practical and creative person

When the Head Line has a slight gentle downward curve, then softness is added to a practical and realistic approach to life. This line shows imagination combined with a realistic attitude. It is perhaps the most common Head Line formation.

Sudden downward curve

When the Head Line is straight for the first half then drops into the Mount of the Moon in later life, it reveals two different life stages. The first is lived in a practical responsible and pragmatic manner. The second stage is much more relaxed and imaginative. Again the shape and overall structure of the hand will guide your interpretation.

Upward curve: The shrewd calculator

A Head Line which curves upward towards the Mercury zone records calculative ability.

When the Head Line curves upwards, there is calculation and shrewdness, as well as business ability and pragmatism. The owner of this line can be mercurial and has an innate

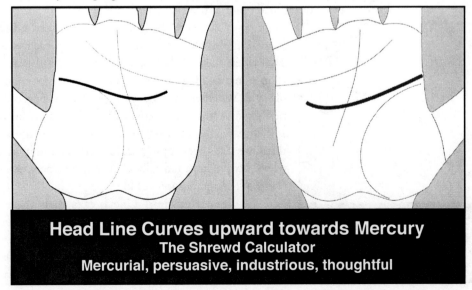

Head Line Curves upward towards Mercury
The Shrewd Calculator
Mercurial, persuasive, industrious, thoughtful

ability to see opportunities for gain in most situations. This person has little time for nebulous theories, except as they might apply to the practical realities of life.

These people can be forceful negotiators if the mounts of Mars are strong, thumb is also strong and Mercury finger long, with a strong political awareness and a good understanding of the consequences of behaviour. If the hands are of a practical type then the focus is upon material gain and industry.

Length

The greater the length of the Head Line the more brain power is at work.

Long Head Lines:

A Head Line which extends to the edge of the palm, or ending beneath the little finger, shows a broad range of interests, and an active mind.

When this line goes to the very edge of the palm, it shows that the mind acts as a filter to emotional expression—feelings have to pass through the brain before they can be expressed. Emotional expression is hindered by mental control. This line has been called 'The Sydney Line'.

Short Head Lines:

A short Head Line is one that does not go any further than half way across the palm. A short Head Line indicates a more narrow range of interests, although not necessarily a low intelligence. Short Head Lines are more common on thick earthy coarse hands with few lines. They are rare and out of place on long flat hands with knuckled fingers and numerous lines, which is the hand of the intelligent communicator, but without the essential ingredient of ample brain power.

A very short Head Line shows that the life focus is upon the outer practical world with little appreciation or understanding of the internal psychological processes.

Breaks

Breaks in the Head Line show breaks or interruptions in mental functioning. These breaks may indicate a sudden shock in the sense of bad news, a head injury affecting the brain, or perhaps

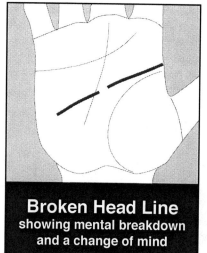

Broken Head Line
showing mental breakdown
and a change of mind

some type of mental breakdown. I have seen a broken Head Line in which the two ends overlap each other in cases where there has been a major change in attitude. This change in attitude has often to do with a major change in lifestyle. Whether this change is positive or negative will be shown by the characteristic of the line after this time, and by the characteristics of the other main lines after this time. This overlapping break is also common in cases where people have radically changed their perspective in terms of their philosophy of life.

When the Head Line breaks then there is a change in the thinking process at the time of the break. Usually this is associated with some shock, nervous breakdown or illness. At the time of the break the gap indicates that the person is unable or has great difficulty in thinking things through clearly. Clarity returns when the Head Line begins anew.

Islands

Islands on the Head Line always indicate a time when an emotional crisis affects the clarity of thinking. Except on the Life Line, islands on any line always indicate some type of emotional disturbance.

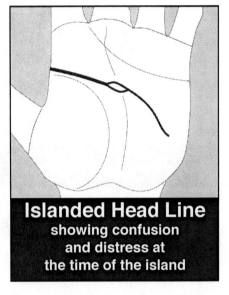

Islanded Head Line
showing confusion
and distress at
the time of the island

Islands on the Head Line are serious as they indicate that the thinking function is impaired for the duration of the island.

The island shows the eruption of repressed pain and hurt rising to the surface of consciousness. Whatever part of our lives the hurt originates from, the time it needs to be dealt with and healed is when the island occurs. Ideally it will have been dealt with before this time, but sometimes other circumstances or priorities prevent us from facing our inner world.

During the time when the island is present, the person is able to see into the depths of their psyche and feel the pain in a powerful way. Such unfamiliar territory can be disturbing to many people. As a consultant it is your responsibility to refer this person to those who are trained to assist in the healing process.

An island on the Head Line always indicates emotional trauma at the time of the island. Islands in palmistry are always associated with negative phenomena, usually of a watery or emotional nature. However this is the line associated with thinking, not feeling, and the presence of an island here indicates that the brain is overwhelmed with feelings that have for too long been repressed, or that some hurt or trauma is too much for the person to cope with and make sense of. The mind is swamped by emotional pain of some type. This indication is always serious and indicates that the person is in urgent need of some therapy or assistance at the time of the island. It is common for people to come to a reading at the time of the island because they are need of help at the time. Because the mind is unable to function properly due to the overwhelming influx of emotions, it is common for the person to report that they are feeling crazy.

Branches

Branches from the Head Line show what is thought about and valued. For example a very straight Head Line with a branch going towards the Mount of Imagination shows a very logical mind that can also be very imaginative, and values creative input. This is also known as the forked head Line.

(See illustration on the next page for branches according to the following letters: A branch going to the Jupiter zone indicates ambitious ideas and idealistic thinking (A). A branch going to the Saturn zone indicates study, organisation, and serious thinking (B). A branch going to the Venus zone indicates artistic ideas and creative thinking (C). A branch going to the Mercury zone indicates business ideas and communication. (D). A branch going to the Moon zone indicates imaginative, mystical ideas (E). *(see illustration on the next page.)*

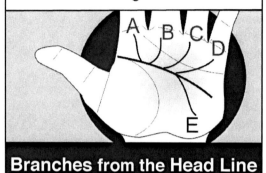

A: Ambitious ideas
B: Study & organisation drive career
C: Artistic, stylistic creative thinking
D: Focus on commerce & exchange
E: Creative & imaginative ideas

Branches from the Head Line

Bars on or Crossing the Head Line

A short line or bar crossing the Head Line indicates an obstacle to be overcome at the time of the bar. Do not confuse a bar with another line that crosses the Head Line. If the Head Line is blocked and finishes at a bar, then this is a serious indication the person reaches some obstacle that they are unable to find a way around—the thinking process is blocked by something that appears insurmountable to the person. This may be a health indication (check the Life Line) or a mental block that requires counselling.

Forked Head Line:

A fork in the Head Line indicates that the person is able to think in two different ways, as indicated by the direction of each fork. For example, if one fork maintains a straight path across the hand, and the other curves downward, then the person is able to think in a logical and practical manner, as well as in an imaginative and creative way.

Under the Saturn finger: However if the downward branch splits early, under the Saturn finger, and terminates on the Mount of the Moon, the sobering and controlling Saturnian influences are not fully integrated within the psyche, indicating that the unchecked imaginative energies can be harmful. The conscious Head Line links with the unconscious energies of the Lunar Mount without any restraining guide.

Fork with branch towards the Saturn finger: If the fork occurs under the Saturn finger with one branch heading towards the Saturn finger, then the nervous system is more delicate. Sometimes this feature is found on intellectually precocious children who overwork the intellect at the expense of other balancing activities.

Under the Venus finger: If the fork occurs under the Venus finger then there is a positive and balanced response to life. Because the line is continuous as it passes under the Jupiter Saturn and Venus fingers, the owner is able to integrate these energies within the psyche.

Weak Head Line

A thin, broken or weak Head Line shows nervous anxiety. This Head Line has been associated with a poor memory. If the Head Line is wavy there is no certainty in the thinking.

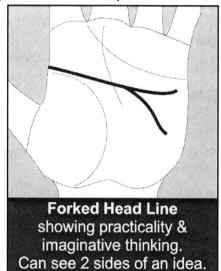

Forked Head Line showing practicality & imaginative thinking. Can see 2 sides of an idea.

Double Head Line

A double Head Line can show two different and distinct ways of looking at a situation. While it usually indicates high intelligence, it can also show confusion.

On a strong hand this duality of thought is not harmful, especially when backed up with a strong thumb. On a weak hand this duality of thought can manifest as a split personality, as though the two hemispheres of the brain are in contest. Otherwise on a weak hand it will manifest as changeability, vacillation, changing opinions and actions which are contrary to stated beliefs.

Closing towards the Heart Line

When the upward curve of the Head Line narrows the gap between the Heart Line before the line curves back downwards, emotions have a strong influence on the thought process. If the deflection occurs early under the Saturn finger, then the emotional effects will be felt between the late teens and mid thirties. Because the Head Line is drawn towards the Saturn zone, a sense of duty or responsibility or requirement to study is likely to be the emotional driving force.

If the upward bulge occurs later in life, under the Venus finger, then there will be an emotional pull towards art or skilful display.

If the Heart Line is the stronger of the two lines, then sentiment will always dominate the thinking process. If it is the Head Line which is stronger, there will be an internal battle between the heart and the head, with associated distress and confusion.

Crossing the Heart Line

This is a most unnatural and dangerous feature. The crossing of primary lines has been associated with sudden death, although this will not be the case with the Saturn line crossing the Head and Heart Lines.

If the Head Line crosses the Heart Line the Head Line will be short, it will allow the emotional forces and other desires to dominate the personality without the guidance of reason.

If this line ends in a cross or star then it is a serious indication of possible sudden death, the causes for which should be explored and removed.

Head Line Joining the Heart Line

This extra short Heart Line shows rational judgement totally overcome by sentiment. The personality will be at the mercy of its passions with no rational control.

If the hands reveal strong physical drives and passions, this person might be a menace to society.

Dating the Head Line

The Head Line is dated using the traditional system from 0 - 72 years of age. Adjustments can be made using an 84 or 96 age system to take account of longer life spans in the modern age. However I recommend the 72 year system as it does seem to be very effective for most people until at least 50 years of age.

Draw an imaginary line down from between the middle of the Saturn and Venus fingers to the centre of the wrist. This is 36 years of age. Divide the rest of the line up proportionately, beginning with 0 just above the thumb.

Questions to Test Your Understanding
(see Page 155 for answers)

Are the following statements true or false?

1: When the Head Line curves steeply into the Mount of the Moon logic prevails.

2: A Head Line that curves upward at the end shows calculation and business acumen.

3: A Head Line that begins high on the Jupiter mount shows pride, leadership capacity, and impulsive self expression.

  4. On a thick and coarse earthy hand a steeply curving Head Line shows imagination.

  5. The Head Line which begins inside the Life Line on the Mount of Outer Mars shows creativity.

Lesson 21

The Heart Line

The ancient art of palmistry has a lot to say about romance in your life. Engraved on the palm are lines which reveal your style of loving, times of contentment and times of heartache. These lines can also be used to assess the style of your potential partners, and to assess compatibility between the two of you.

The most important indicator of your love life is the upper horizontal line on the palm, usually called "the heart line". This line has to do with matters of the heart, your feelings and how you express them to others.

The Heart Line is the upper transverse line of the palm. It records feelings, in the sense of how they are expressed to other people, and how they are experienced. This line also records the physical condition of the heart and circulation.

The Meaning Of The Heart Line

The meaning of the Heart Line is found from the sides of the palm it links together - the inner world of fantasies and dreams (the side of the palm beneath the little finger), and the outer world where other people are encountered (the area of the palm on the thumb side of the hand). From this we can see that the Heart Line has to do with how inner feelings are expressed to other people.

The Heart Line links the functions of the zones of the upper palm which lie beneath the 4 fingers. These are the Jupiter Zone (pride, honour, dignity, loyalty and high ideals), the Saturn Zone (pragmatism, sensuality, responsibility, conscience), the Venus Zone (optimism and beauty), and the Mercury Zone (communication of ideas and feelings, and commerce).

The Heart Line shows which qualities are valued. The type of hand on which it is found will show how these values find expression.

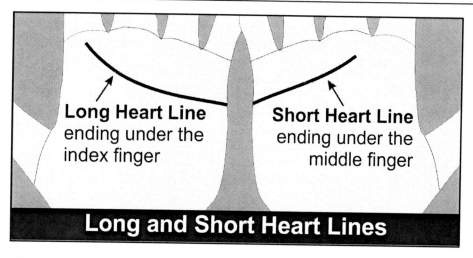

Long and Short Heart Lines

The Heart Line can be read in 2 directions

1. Beginning on the outer (thumb side) of the hand and reading towards the little finger shows how feelings are expressed in relationships. This is the 'normal' way the Heart Line is read.

2. Beginning beneath the little finger and reading towards the thumb side of the palm shows the earliest experiences of being nurtured. This is particularly useful for establishing how much love was experienced in childhood. However while in theory it is possible to read the Heart Line in this direction, I found that its main practical use is for reading the influences of childhood and early adulthood, under the Mercury finger.

Heart Line types
The Idealistic Heart Line

A Heart Line which is very long and runs to the edge of the palm under the index finger, shows an idealist. This is the trusting and sentimental person, prepared to sacrifice personal needs for their partner. Principles are very high, and the same is expected of others. The partner is put on a pedestal, and can do no wrong. The down side to all of this is disappointment when the partner's standards do not live up to expectation.

A Heart Line can be considered idealistic if it ends anywhere under the first finger. These idealistic feelings go to extremes if the line ends at the edge of the hand, or on the finger itself. A long Heart Line shows strong feelings, and the focus of these feelings will be described by the type of hand on which they are found.

Ending under the Jupiter finger shows altruistic idealism, pride and sentimentality. There is an over emphasis upon trust, loyalty and sincerity when this line ends close to the index finger. Here the partner is placed upon an idealistic pedestal and adored in a sentimental manner. When this long line is pronounced there is blindness to the frailties of the partner and those close to the heart. Revelation of their partner's weakness can come as a shock and result in a reversal of loyalty. These qualities are moderated when the line ends low on this zone or ends close to the middle finger.

Such a long heart line can also show a judgemental attitude as well as anger, especially if the lines on the palm are very red.

Ending at the outer edge of the hand indicates that adoration and loyalty to a cause are pushed to extremes. This person is 'all heart'. Sentiment, romantic ideals and emotions overshadow commonsense and logical foresight. Verity says that this "...creates a barrier effect", giving impulsive feelings unnatural predominance over the thinking processes. I have observed that this line indicates a very humanitarian outlook and a sense of universal brotherhood. Ending under the Jupiter finger shows altruistic idealism, pride and sentimentality.

If the Idealistic heart Line is found on the sensitive emotional hand (soft, slender and supple), then emotions go to extremes. This is a person who is unusually sentimental in matters of the heart, devoted to the partner to the point of adoration, and willing to sacrifice their own needs in order to make their loved ones happy. They are likely to be blind to the faults of those they love.

If this unusually long Heart Line is found upon the thoughtful communicator's hand (knotty, flat and firm) then principles will be all-important. This person's skill with words and general persuasiveness will be used to benefit loved ones. Belief systems will be built around what is right, just and ideal. Intellectual communicators with such a long Heart Line will blindly devote their life to a cause which they believe is right and ideal in their eyes.

If this line is found on the outgoing practical person's hand (broad, firm and well padded), then their outgoing social nature will be expressed in a very sentimental way. This person will be generous, loyal, and devoted. Because their firm hands do not indicate a ready emotional response, the strong emotional content revealed by this long Heart Line will be expressed through a sense of camaraderie, with the outgoing and generous social nature strongly emphasised in all areas of life.

The Pragmatic Heart Line

If your heart line finishes under the Saturn finger, then you are the pragmatist in love. You prefer to consider the practical realities of any potential partnership in terms of what you stand to gain. You will consider the short term gain regarding sensual and sexual satisfaction, and you will also consider the long term financial prospects. If the hands are flat (very little padding) and hard, then the mental focus will be pragmatic and realistic, with little warmth or sentimentality. If your hands are soft with lots of padding, then you will be very sensual and self indulgent. If the hands are broad and firm, then an industrious hard-working nature will be directed towards clear goals, unfettered by sentimentality.

The Balanced Heart Line

It is common to find that the heart line ends somewhere between the Jupiter and Saturn fingers. This shows a natural balance between the extremes of idealism and pragmatism. Common sense prevails. Sentiment, emotion, and pragmatism are all motivating forces. Branches from the Heart Line going to the Jupiter Zone show add sentimentality and idealism. Branches ending in the area under the Saturn finger above the heart line add pragmatism and materialism.

The Physical Heart Line

If the Heart Line is steeply curving then there is a need for lots of cuddles and physical closeness. The sensation of skin against skin is needed on a regular basis to feel content. Sensual and sexual expression is important.

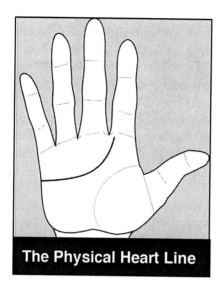

The Physical Heart Line

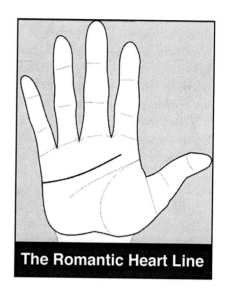

The Romantic Heart Line

The Romantic Heart Line

If the Heart Line follows a relatively straight path then it is 'the vibes' that play such an important role in romantic encounters. The music, the 'atmosphere', and the mood are important. The state of mind is critical. This has sometimes been called 'the Mental Heart Line', because it is closer to the Head Line. Emotional responses depend very much on the mental state. When stress is present, then it won't matter how enthusiastic the partner may be. Being 'in the right mood' is so important for those with the Romantic Heart Line. Because this line is in close proximity to the Head Line it shows a need for acknowledgement and recognition in reward for caring and helping others. This Heart Line shows the need for verbal appreciation.

The 6 basic Heart Line types

The combination of the various Heart Lines described so far give us six possible types. The first two that have already been discussed, both end in the area beneath the gap between the Jupiter and Saturn fingers. Each combines commonsense with their basic traits. They are:

1. **The Balanced Physical Heart Line and**

2. **The Balanced Romantic Heart Line.**

Each shows balance in the sense of being able to include both high principles and pragmatic commonsense in their emotional involvement with others.

The other four combinations result from combining the Idealistic Heart Line with the Physical and Romantic Heart Lines, and from combining the Pragmatic Heart Line with the Physical and Romantic Heart Lines.

These four combinations are: 3. The Idealistic Physical Heart Line, 4. The Idealistic Romantic Heart Line, 5. The Pragmatic Physical Heart Line, and 6. The Pragmatic Romantic Heart Line.

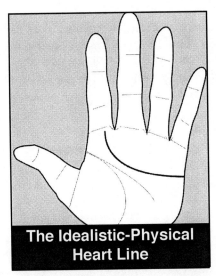

The Idealistic-Physical Heart Line

The Idealistic-Romantic Heart Line

3. The Idealistic Physical Heart Line: This Heart Line indicates lofty ideals regarding physical form, appearance, sensual and sexual satisfaction. The owner of these hands will be frustrated if the person they put their faith in does not respond with cuddles, physical warmth and sexual activity. They will want to offer warmth and physical affection to those they love.

4. The Idealistic Romantic Heart Line: Here the ideals are centred upon romantic visions, with a strong need to share feelings of tenderness in an atmosphere that reflects their loving appreciation. Faith and adoration are combined with romance. This Heart Line is 'more at home' on the Sensitive Emotional Hand. The basic need shown by this hand type is to nurture, express affection and emotional sensitivities.

5. The Pragmatic Physical Heart Line: This Heart Line type combines the qualities of pragmatism with sensuality. The result is someone who loves sensuality and sex, and will seek relationships for this purpose. Relationships may also be sought for other reasons, such as financial or material reward, with physical and sensual indulgence pursued as the opportunity presents itself.

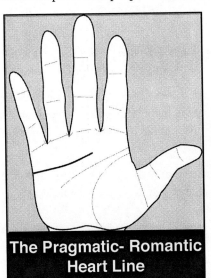

The Pragmatic- Romantic Heart Line

6. The Pragmatic Romantic Heart Line: This apparently contradictory and rare combination indicates someone who finds pleasure in romantic interludes. This person is both realistic and mentally stimulated by the "romantic atmosphere" of poetry, music and lovely surroundings, when in the company of someone they find attractive. Pleasure is found "in the moment". Loyalty is replaced by pragmatism.

The character of the Heart Line

Changes in the character of the Heart Line show fluctuations in the feelings. Many palmists also believe that changes in the character of the Heart Line also show changes in the action of the physical heart.

A thinning of the Heart Line indicates less feeling at the time of the thinning, and a weaker action of the physical heart. Indications on other lines may suggest reasons for this thinning.

A deepening or thickening of the Heart Line shows that strong feelings are felt and expressed towards others, as well as a stronger action of the heart. The zone nearest the deepening of the Heart Line will indicate the nature of the deepened feelings.

A Heart Line which stops and starts show that feelings run hot and cold, and indicates a suspect heart. This person will be moody and unpredictable.

Defections of the Heart Line

1. Towards a zone:

Deflections of the Heart Line towards a zone indicate an attraction for people and things associated with the qualities represented by the zone. For example a deflection of the line towards the Saturn Zone shows an attraction towards serious and authoritive types. Rising towards the Mercury Zone shows a love of money making or an attraction towards business people.

2. Away from a zone:

Deflections away from a zone show an aversion to people associated with the qualities of that zone. For example if the Heart Line drops beneath the Venus finger and then rises to resume its previous level, then there is a dislike of artistic, creative or "showy" people.

Interpreting the Heart Line
from its beginning under the Mercury finger:

A tassel at the beginning (numerous small lines) shows vulnerability and openness as a child. This is the most common and most healthy beginning for the Heart Line. It shows nurture and input from a wide variety of sources.

Beginning closed with few or no branches shows little input for nurturing others as a child, resulting in a more closed-in attitude to others and a tougher approach to life.

Beginning higher on the Mercury Zone shows a love of industry, money making, and communication. On an intellectual communicator's hands this indicates great shrewdness and persuasiveness. In all cases love is conditional upon reward or exchange, with a strong emphasis upon communication skills.

Beginning on the Zone of Venus indicates that love must be beautifully packaged. Beauty is the great motivating factor. This beginning also suggests a weak heart.

Heart Line Endings

Ending on the Zone of Venus indicates a lack of warmth except where beauty and its appreciation is concerned. This is a very short Heart Line and indicates possible heart problems. Short-Heart Lines show coldness and are said by some palmists to be associated with health problems.

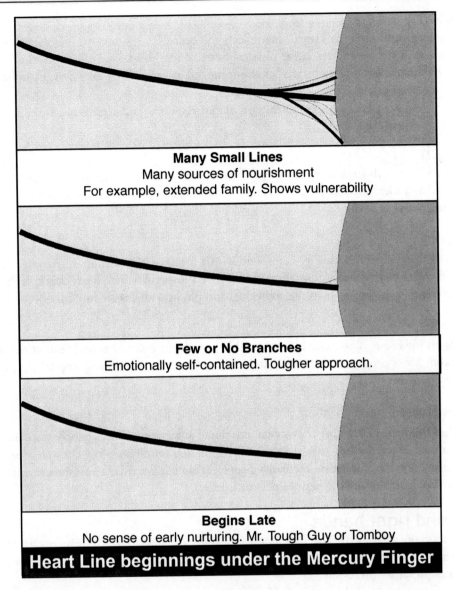

Many Small Lines
Many sources of nourishment
For example, extended family. Shows vulnerability

Few or No Branches
Emotionally self-contained. Tougher approach.

Begins Late
No sense of early nurturing. Mr. Tough Guy or Tomboy

Heart Line beginnings under the Mercury Finger

Branches ending beneath the Jupiter and Saturn fingers: It is normal for the heart Line to terminate in 1 or 2 or possibly 3 or 4 branches beneath the Jupiter and Saturn fingers and between these fingers. This multiple terminations show a balance between common sense and idealism, high values and utility. The strongest branch will indicate the strongest feeling. Multiple endings also suggest a rich emotional life with a wide variety of affectionate expressions.

Ending on the Head Line shows that mental calculation overshadows sentiment and romance. Here the "head rules the heart". It is important to assess the relative strengths of the Head Line and the Heart Line to establish the strongest influence.

Ending on the Outer Mars Mount shows aggressive feelings alternating with timidity. This is fortunately a very rare formation.

Anatomy

On an anatomical level the Heart Line reflects the heart. Breaks or disturbances on the Heart Line may indicate weaknesses in the physical heart. If the Heart Line is composed of multiple islands, or has many stops and starts, or major breaks, or varies in its thickness, then the operation of the heart or circulation may be suspect.

From a legal perspective it is important that you do not offer medical advice, but instead suggest a medical check-up.

Length

A Heart Line which runs from one edge of that palm to the other indicates someone 'with a big heart' and idealistic notions. Conversely a short Heart Line indicates someone with little emotional warmth to offer.

Breaks

Breaks in the Heart Line usually correspond with a break in relationship or marriage and correspond with a 'heart-break'. Sometimes this break corresponds with a heart attack. If the Heart Line overlaps at the breaks then the emotional and physical effects are minimised.

Islands

Islands on the Heart Line indicate emotional heart-ache or emotional problems at the time of the island. Most people have 1 or 2 islands on the Heart Line, showing emotional sensitivity and involvement.

Branches

Branches from the Heart Line show what emotional attraction towards people associated with the qualities represented by that zone on which the line terminates. For example Venus zone shows attraction towards artists or creative people. A branch towards Saturn shows an attraction toward people in authority or serious personalities.

Left and right hands

It is important to compare the two hands and note any important differences. If the Heart Lines have a different shape then there will be differences between what is desired and the strategies used to satisfy this desire.

For example, if the romantic Heart Line is found on the inner hand and the physical Heart Line on the outer hand, then physical love making may be initiated with the intention of having a romantic experience. This might be very confusing and frustrating to the partner. Conversely if the physical Heart Line is found on the inner hand and the romantic Heart Line is found on the outer hand, then romantic activity is initiated with the intention of satisfying the physical needs.

There are many possible combinations of the different Heart Lines. Logic and common sense will guide your interpretations.

A further more advanced study involves comparing the different Heart Lines of a couple in order to understand the dynamics between them and hopefully find a path to mutual fulfillment. That study is outside the scope of these lessons and is fertile ground for enthusiastic palmists to explore in the future.

Timing the Heart Line

The traditional system of timing the heart Line for relationship events that I was taught begins with 0 and ends with 72. The intersection of the Heart Line with an imaginary line is drawn down vertically between the Saturn and Venus fingers is 36 years of age.

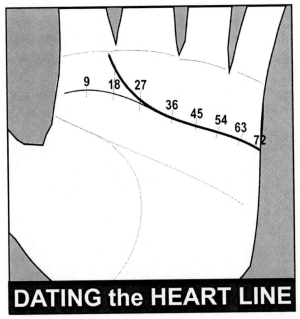

DATING the HEART LINE

On the thumb side of the palm halfway between this imaginary line and the edge of the palm is 18 years of age, and halfway between this imaginary line and the edge of the palm under the Mercury finger is 54 years of age.

I do of course understand that in modern times that people in Western countries and newly developed countries frequently live to the late 80's and early 90's. However for some reason this system of timing the hands seems to work very well, especially for clients up to the age of 50, which includes most clients. I have heard reports that some palmists use a timing scale from 0 to 84 years of age with success.

The Heart Line can also be timed in the opposite direction using the traditional system mentioned above, to show how the person experiences nurturing. Using the same technique as described above but in reverse, beginning at the edge of the palm under the Mercury finger, the halfway point between the Saturn and Venus fingers shows events at 36 years of age, the first quarter mark at 18 years of age, and the last quarter mark (at the intersection of an imaginary line drawn down between the Jupiter and Saturn fingers), shows 54 years of age.

In my experience reading the Heart line in this direction is only useful for the first third of life, up to about 24 years of age. Islands on the Heart Line under the Mercury finger show childhood trauma. Sometimes, but not always, this trauma may be the result of sexual interference. I strongly advise against mentioning the possibility of sexual interference directly to a client, as I believe it is wrong to implant suggestions about something that may not have occurred, as such a suggestion can create a fantasy in the client's mind and consequently have a very negative impact on present relationships, especially if it turns out to be incorrect. However an island in this area is, in my experience, a sure indicator of childhood trauma of some type.

Questions to Test Your Understanding
(see Page 155 for answers)

Are the following statements true or false?

1: A Heart Line that curves steeply shows it is 'the vibes' which are important in romantic encounters.

2: The Heart Line which ends under the Saturn finger shows a pragmatic approach to love.

3: A Heart Line which ends under the Jupiter finger shows artistic creativity.

4. A Heart Line which deflects towards the Venus zone indicates a love of artists.

5. The organ of the body the Heart Line is most associated with is the spine.

Lesson 22

The Combination Line

In approximately ten percent of the population the Head and Heart Lines are fused into one line. This line is often given the unfortunate name of the 'simian line' because it is found on the hands of apes. It is also one of the identifying markers of Down Syndrome (Trisomy 21). However it is also found on the hands of highly intelligent people and also many people with average intelligence and abilities. It is discussed here because it deserves special treatment as a main line of the hand as it is found on the hands of so many people from diverse backgrounds.

When the Heart Line and the Head Line are fused into one line the feelings and the thoughts have to 'move' through the same channel. When these energies travel together in harmony they provide a very powerful focus. When they are not travelling in harmony the mental and emotional expression can be erratic. Consequently the Combination Line shows someone who can be highly focused and concentrated at some times and also erratic at other times. There will be shifts from high focus to unpredictable expression of feelings and thoughts.

The important question is: What is being focused? For the answer to this question you must look to the overall hand type and structure. If the hand structure shows a physical and instinctive response to life, then it will be the animal instincts that become amplified. If the hand structure reveals a strong intellect, then the mental concentration and focus will be a central feature of this person's life. As always with hand reading, you must match the lines with the hands on which they are found.

Sometimes there is a clearly marked Head Line and Heart Line with a very strong link between the two. This formation functions as a 'watered-down' Combination Line but with less emphasis on high focus and erratic confusion. It shows a blend of the high focus associated with the Combination line, with the capacity for the thinking and feeling processes to function somewhat independently.

Head or Heart?

Rarely, howeve, do we see a single straight line across the palm. Generally there are fragments of the Head Line or Heart Line either joined to the Combination Line or separated from it. Sometimes these fragments or partial formations of the Head Line or Heart Line will show by their number or depth which function dominates.

Sometimes the Combination Line will be located closer to the normal position of the Head Line or the Heart Line. Its proximity to the normal position of either of these lines shows its bias. If it is close to the normal position of the Head Line, then the Combination Line will show that in the struggle between thoughts and feelings, thoughts dominate. Look to see what type of hand this line is found upon. For example if thoughts dominate on a hand characterised by sensitive emotional responses, there is an internal conflict. However if thoughts dominate on the savvy communicator's hand, then the internal energies are congruent, albeit with some inner tension.

Sometimes the bias is revealed by one end of the Combination Line being noticeably thicker. If the end under the Mercury Finger is thick, then it is intense feelings that dominate, as this is normally the beginning point of the Heart Line. The intense feelings may reduce 'common sense' and attract accidents. Again it is important to match the line with the hand structure.

Left or Right Hand?

If the Combination Line is found on both hands there will be a strong focus mixed with periods of some inner tension/confusion. However if the Combination Line is found on only one hand, which is more common, then it is necessary to distinguish between the inner and outer worlds.

If the Combination Line is found on the inner hand, then a lot of attention is focused on the inner needs, home life and relationship. The outer hand will show how this concentrated focus and tension will be resolved. Look for other differences between the hands, and also at the character of the Head Line and Heart Line. For example, if there is a wide gap between the beginning of the Head Line and Life Line on the outer hand, and a strong link between the two on the inner hand, then the inner tensions are resolved or dealt with by becoming more open and spontaneous.

The character of the Head Line and Heart Line on the hand on which they are separate will assist your interpretation. For example if the Combination Line is on the outer hand and the inner hand shows a very long Heart Line, then there will be an intense focus on the resolution of altruistic feelings. Look to the rest of the hand to evaluate what these strong feelings may relate to, and above all, listen to your client.

If the Combination Line is found on the inner hand and on the outer hand a steeply sloping Head Line goes down into the Mount of the Moon, then imaginative, creative, and perhaps theatrical outlets will be sought to resolve inner tensions. If in this case there is little evidence of creative energy shown elsewhere on the hands, then this sloping Head Line will find expression in technical innovation and unusual theoretical constructs.

There is not the space here to list all the possible variations of the Combination Line being found on the one hand and features on the other. Hand reading requires the ability to interpret a combination of qualities based on a knowledge of fundamental principles and common sense. This skill improves with practice, although not everybody has a natural talent in this area.

Combining with Hand Type

The best way to interpret how the Combination Line functions is to match it with the type of hand on which it is found.

Fire Hand: The Fire Hand has a long palm (usually fleshy) and relatively short fingers. A well padded palm will provide high energy and the short fingers will show the need to express this energy spontaneously. If the Combination Line is found on these hands then the need for action and spontaneous expression can be frustrated by the internal 'conversation' between the heart and the head. If this hand is also inflexible then the internal frustration will be amplified, resulting in pent-up energy exploding in fiery outbursts. Flexibility of the hands will defuse some of this inner tension.

Earth Hand: If this line is found on the earthy hand (broad heavy inflexible hand with few lines and coarse skin), there will be a sustained physical response to life's challenges, with periods of 'time-out' when the mind needs to rest and integrate impressions and experiences. As this hand type does not show a strong intellectual component, the responses will be instinctive and less conscious.

Sensitive Emotional Hands: If the Combination Line is found on the sensitive emotional hand (soft supple and slender), then the challenge will be to make sense of emotional experiences. This can indicate periods of confusion when the rational mind wrestles with the less conscious emotional mind. Generally the emotional mind will win as the emotions dominate on this hand type. It is important for people with combination lines on sensitive emotional hands to have pre-planned strategies to enable them to cope at these confusing times.

Intellectual Communicator's Hand: When the Combination Line is found on the intellectual communicator's hand (knotty fingers and a flat and inflexible hand), then the challenge will be to express and integrate emotions. On this hand it is the intellect which rules, with little emotional expression or comprehension available. One of the features of the intellectual communicator's hand is the need to withdraw from human society and spend time with nature, especially in times of stress and hurt. If this hand contains the Combination Line then this need may be exaggerated.

Questions to Test Your Understanding
(see Page 155 for answers)

Are the following statements true or false?
1: The Combination Line is a fusion of the Head Line and the Heart Line.
2: The Combination Line is most often found on the left hand.
3: The Combination Line is often referred to as 'the simian line'.
4. If the Combination Line sits close to the normal position of the Head Line it shows emotional expressiveness.
5. The Combination Line shows intense focus alternating with erratic periods.

Lesson 23

The Saturn Line

How to identify the Saturn Line

The Saturn Line is distinguished from other lines by 3 criteria:

> 1. It must be a vertical line;
>
> 2. It must pass through the centre of the palm; and
>
> 3. It must head toward the middle (Saturn) finger.
>   If a line meets these three criteria then it can be called a Saturn Line.

The Meaning of the Saturn Line

In palmistry the planet Saturn represents manifestation on the physical plane and the material reality of one's life. It is also associated with the 'super-conscious' of Freudian psychology - that part of our psyche which judges what is permissible and what is not. It is our conscience, formed by the punishments and rewards metered out in our formative years.

In the light of this interpretation it is easy to understand how Saturn in modern astrology has come to be associated with fears.

The interpretation of this line follows the simple logic of palmistry which says that the meaning of a line is can be understood by the areas of the palm it links together. This line links the base of the palm to the top of the palm beneath the middle finger. The base of the palm represents the unconscious mind and its needs for physical fulfilment, and the area beneath the middle finger represents material gain, career and social engagement.

Basically the Saturn Line shows how the inside of a person relates to the outer material reality.

This line shows how well the inner drives find fulfilment in social and physical reality. It shows how well you are able to manifest and integrate your underlying drives into the physical and social world. It could also be called "The Integration Line" or "The Career Line". The

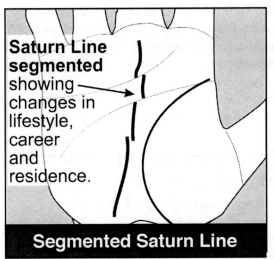

Saturn Line segmented showing changes in lifestyle, career and residence.

Segmented Saturn Line

Saturn Line is primarily a recorder of social adaptability and the ability to find a meaningful role in society. For many people this role manifests through their career.

The traditional name of the Saturn Line is 'The Fate Line' which is misleading as this line has little to do with fate. It is also unfortunate as the name implies a sense of mystery and lack of choice.

In these lessons this line will be referred to as 'The Saturn Line', reflecting astrological thought which sees Saturn as the ruler of the Midheaven which is the career point in the horoscope. Saturn is also lord of the earthly realm and deals with physical reality. If you have knowledge of astrology you might be interested to note that the base of the palm and the top of the palm beneath the middle finger accurately reflect the IC and Midheaven respectively. This line reflects the connection between the home base (IC) and career (Midheaven).

On a practical level we can safely interpret this as a career line. It should be pointed out that motherhood and parenting are examples of a role which, while not commonly referred to as a career, is one of the most important and most demanding careers anyone could choose.

On a general level this line also shows lifestyle, as our lifestyle often is centred around our career or main role in society.

The meaning of the Saturn Line is derived from the fact that it links the base of the palm with the top of the palm. Thus it records how the inner feelings find satisfaction and fulfilment in the outer world of material and social reality.

The area beneath the middle finger is commonly referred to as "The Saturn Mount" in traditional palmistry literature. However because in truth it is not actually a mount but a depression between two mounts, I shall refer to it here as "The Saturn Zone". The finger above it is traditionally referred to as the Saturn Finger.

Combining with hand types

The Saturn Line is associated with one's career (Outer hand), and one's sense of direction (Inner hand).

The meaning of the Saturn line will depend so much on the type of hand on which it is found. *For example on a hand which shows a strong intellectual bias, the Inner hand will show changes in philosophy, religion or ideals. It has much to do with one's satisfaction with financial wellbeing.

*On a sensitive emotional hand the inner hand will reflect contentment with domestic and relationship arrangements.

While taking into account the underlying hand structure, we can generally say that the inner hand shows the sense of direction and contentment with one's financial and social position, and the outer hand shows changes in address and career. The word 'address' is used here in the sense of social position and physical address.

Another important meaning associated with this line is that it records social adaptability and acceptance - the sense of position and acceptance within one's community or social group. Thus a strong Saturn Line is often found on the hands of mothers and others who play strong supportive roles within the community, but who may not have a career in the traditional sense.

When this line is absent there is little or no sense of community, and neither is there a conscience in the sense of social duty or obligation. It is common for those who are incarcerated to have no Saturn Line.

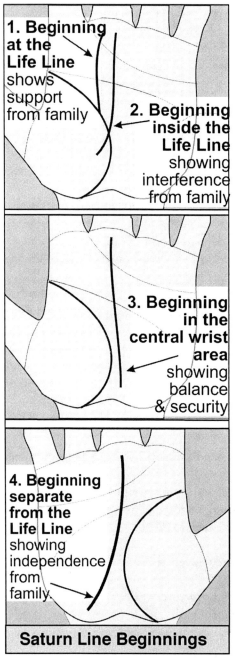

1. Beginning at the Life Line shows support from family

2. Beginning inside the Life Line showing interference from family

3. Beginning in the central wrist area showing balance & security

4. Beginning separate from the Life Line showing independence from family

Saturn Line Beginnings

The Saturn Line has 4 common beginning points:

1. Beginning from the Life Line

This beginning shows early support from the family. Up to the point where the Saturn Line separates from the Life Line, the person spends most of their time trying to satisfy the wishes of others. At the point where the Saturn Line separates, the person breaks away to achieve independence. Because the Life Line reflects feelings of love and vitality, this feature shows that the person draws upon the loving approval of others for success.

2. Beginning inside the Life Line

This beginning shows that family influences were experienced as restrictive and coercive. At the point where the Saturn Line separates, the person breaks away from this restriction to achieve independence.

3. Beginning from the central wrist area

This beginning shows early and successful interaction with others. This indicates confidence and security. However this successful beginning is lessened if there are small interference lines coming in from the wrist area at the base of the palm. These lines indicate a sense of being smothered by pressure from others to perform or behave ways that satisfies their projected needs, but stifles the child's self expression.

4. Beginning from the Mount of the Moon

This beginning shows feeling independent at an early age, and opposition to the wishes of the parents or other caretakers. It also suggests that people outside the family circle play a positive and influential role early in the person's life.

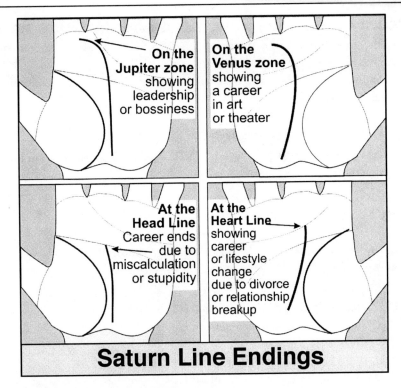

On the Jupiter zone showing leadership or bossiness

On the Venus zone showing a career in art or theater

At the Head Line Career ends due to miscalculation or stupidity

At the Heart Line showing career or lifestyle change due to divorce or relationship breakup

Saturn Line Endings

Endings Of The Saturn Line

The normal ending of the Saturn Line is in the area of the palm between the Heart Line and the base of the middle finger. This is the zone of physical manifestation, material gain, and reflects the physical and social environment in which we live.

Ending beneath the Jupiter Finger shows ambitious tendencies, particularly later in life. This ending shows a desire for prominence and leadership on the passive hand, and on the active hand indicates the attainment of position and leadership. On a hand type which shows little inclination for career or worldly success such as the romantic emotional hand (soft supple slender hand), this ending shows bossiness.

Ending beneath the Venus finger suggests a career in the arts or at least involving the arts in some way. On a hand where the primary inclinations are towards business and financial gain, this may indicate someone who deals or trades in works of art.

Ending at the Head Line suggests some type of miscalculation that brings the career to an end if there are no other Saturn Lines. This is based on the fact that the Head Line has to do with thinking, and the Saturn Line stopping indicates an end to the career. Some type of change of mind or attitude results in a complete change of direction. However if there is another Saturn line beginning from the head Line or further up the palm, studious or intellectual endeavours lead to a new career.

Ending at the Heart Line suggests that some type of relationship breakup has the effect of bringing the career or lifestyle to an end. If this ending is found only on the passive hand, then the sense of purpose or direction is lost, even though it is possible to continue the performance of this role as before.

If this ending is found only on the active hand, then for some reason it is impossible to continue even though the desire is still strong.

The Saturn Line on the Inner hand and the Outer hand

The Saturn Line on the inner hand shows one's perspective or sense of direction and purpose, as well as feelings of fulfilment regarding one's social life.

The Saturn Line on the outer hand shows how the feelings of "fitting-in" are satisfied in profession and lifestyle.

Character of the Saturn Line

Breaks in the Saturn Line on the passive hand show a change in outlook upon life, a change in our sense of direction.

On the active hand breaks indicate a change of career or a change in social position. Islands on the Saturn Line indicate dissatisfaction with the career. On the passive hand islands show unhappiness with career, and suggest deep emotional disturbance. This is often found on the hands of those who feel trapped because of other responsibilities, such as the demands of motherhood over-riding a sense of grief about loss of freedom.

Islands and breaks on and Saturn Line

Islands on the passive hand indicate general confusion or dissatisfaction with one's general direction, philosophy or social position.

On the outer hand islands show a career problem.

Breaks on the inner hand suggest a change of outlook and a change in one's sense of direction.

On the outer hand breaks show times of unemployment, or inactivity. These times can be used to study or travel. Other negative indications such as cross bars, crosses or interruptions from the other minor lines show disruptive influences.

Dating the Saturn Line

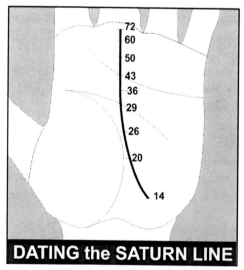

DATING the SATURN LINE

At the point where the Saturn Line crosses the head Line is approximately 29 years of age. This point correlates very well with what astrologers call 'the first Saturn return', which is when the planet Saturn returns to its natal position for the first time. It is a time of maturity, of 'growing up', and facing the reality of responsibility, and most people go through an important change in their lifestyle or career at this point.

The actual beginning of the Saturn Line is difficult to define. In theory it begins at zero, but because most people do not make independent choices until at least their early teens, the beginning of this line can be dated at approx 14 years of age, which is half a Saturn cycle.

From the time when the Saturn Line crosses the Head Line until it terminates at the top of the palm the Head Line is dated from 29 years of age to 72 years of age. You will notice that the space on the hands allotted for this period is disproportionate. The space from the base of the palm up until the Head Line comprises more than half the length of the palm, yet it is allotted only 30 years. However I can say from extensive personal experience reading hundreds of hands that dating this point at 29 years of age works very well. The reason why such a disproportionate area of the palm is allotted to only the first 29 years perhaps reflects the importance of this period from a physical and psychological perspective.

The space from the Head Line to the Heart Line (29 – 43 years of age) is allotted the next 14 years approximately. It is difficult to be exact and it also depends on how high or low the Heart Line sits on the palm.

From the Heart Line to the top of the palm is the last period of life. In modern time it is true that people are living into their mid eighties and early nineties. You may wish to experiment with dating this period to 87 years of age (3 Saturn returns). However with such a small space on the palm it is difficult to be precise.

Examples

In the illustration at right, the Saturn Line beginning at A shows family support for a new career in the mid thirties. At this time the client resigned from his clerical job and became a property developer.

The Saturn Line beginning at B shows family interference. It crosses the Life Line in the late twenties when the client finally overcame family opposition and joined the army. Note that the line is dated from when it crossed the Life Line.

Line C begins on the Mount of the Moon, revealing a career choice that is independent of family tradition. For generations the family ran a grocery business, but she studied fashion design from a young age and eventually became very successful.

Also note that the Saturn Line begins on the left hand at A in the mid teens and moves up the palm in an unsteady fashion until it dissipates around the Heart Line, in the early 40's. The same pattern is replicated on the right hand where it begins at C. These prints show someone with a lot of nervous energy and stress without a strong sense of direction or an active role in life.

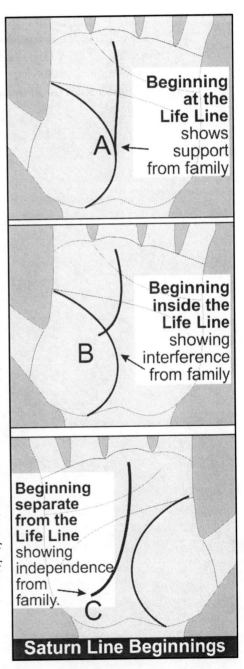

Beginning at the Life Line shows support from family

Beginning inside the Life Line showing interference from family

Beginning separate from the Life Line showing independence from family.

Saturn Line Beginnings

Questions to Test Your Understanding
(see Page 155 for answers)

Are the following statements true or false?

1. The Saturn Line runs vertically through the palm towards the Saturn finger.
2. A Saturn Line which begins on the Mount of the Moon shows strong assertive skills.
3. A Saturn Line that begins inside the Life Line shows domination by family in the choice of career. Shows domination by family in the choice of career.
4. If the Combination Line sits close to the normal position of the Head Line it shows emotional expressiveness.
5. The Combination shows intense focus alternating with erratic periods.

Lesson 24

Branches From the Main Lines

At this point in the book we have covered all the main lines. In this chapter we revisit the main lines for a refresher on branches from these lines.

Branches from the main lines act as secondary lines which record the development and further refinement of the main lines.

Branches from the Life Line

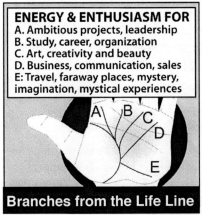

ENERGY & ENTHUSIASM FOR
A. Ambitious projects, leadership
B. Study, career, organization
C. Art, creativity and beauty
D. Business, communication, sales
E: Travel, faraway places, mystery, imagination, mystical experiences

Branches from the Life Line

The Life Line represents vitality, passion and enthusiasm, and is itself empowered by the Sun Mount. If the Sun Mount is full and wide there exists powerful reserves available to energise the Life Line. If the Sun Mount is flat and narrow then the Life Line receives little energy. Your assessment of the strength of the Life Line will be based on the relative strengths of the Sun Mount and Life Lines on both hands. Remember to compare the relative strengths of these features on both hands. There is little that is black and white in hand analysis – rather most assessments are based on balancing different factors.

The area of the palm on which a branch from the Life Line terminates is invigorated. There is a strong life focus on this area. This area receives a boost of life giving solar energy from the Life Line. It is important to memorize the meaning of the zones of the palm – go back to Section 1 and read the chapter on the Zones of the Palm.

A branch from the Life Line ending on the:

- Jupiter Zone (A) energises pride and idealism and suggests ambition.

- Saturn Line (B) and suggests a strong family influence upon career, study and organising skills.

- Venus Zone (C) shows that feelings for beauty and art are energised by the life force, suggesting some type of talent.

- Mercury Zone (D) shows an aptitude for communication and business.

- Mount of the Moon (E) amplifies the inner yearning for new experiences and usually suggests a wish for travel.

Branches from the Head Line

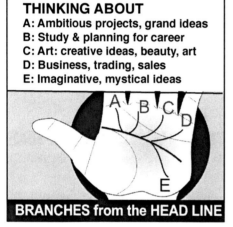

THINKING ABOUT
A: Ambitious projects, grand ideas
B: Study & planning for career
C: Art: creative ideas, beauty, art
D: Business, trading, sales
E: Imaginative, mystical ideas

BRANCHES from the HEAD LINE

The Head Line reflects the thinking process and branches from this line show the direction taken by the thought process. The zone on which the branch terminates describes this process. For example, if a branch from the Head Line terminates on the Venus Zone, then the person thinks about artists or about artistic subjects. It also suggests that the thinking process is in some way creative or artistic. If a branch from the Head Line terminates on the Mount of the Moon then the thinking is more emotional, and is influenced by fantasy, design and superstition. In this case the client thinks about matters which are mystical, imaginative and perhaps poetic.

A branch from the Head Line ending on the:

- Jupiter Zone shows 'bigness of thought', ambitious ideas and thinking about prominent people or principles.

- Saturn Zone functions as a Saturn Line and suggests studious endeavours and serious and responsible mental focus.

- Venus Zone shows thinking about beauty and art, creative thinking, and perhaps thinking about creative people.

- Mercury Zone shows thinking about communication and business, and business people.

- Mount of the Moon shows that ideas and images become amplified by emotional reactions and a tendency to exaggerate. The mind travels to 'faraway places'. It is important to assess how far down on the Mount of the Moon this branch terminates. The further the Head Line goes into the Mount of the Moon the stronger is the inclusion of emotional energies into the thinking process.

Branches from the Heart Line

ATTRACTION TOWARDS
A. A noble cause, atruism, loyalty
B. Studious serious, authoritive types
C. Artistic creative people, beauty, art
D. Business people, trading

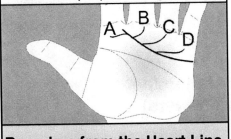

Branches from the Heart Line

The Heart Line records the feelings and emotional attractions. Branches from the Heart Line show feelings which are associated with qualities represented on the area of the palm on which the branch terminates.

- Jupiter Zone: An attraction towards leaders, confident and inspirational people

- Saturn Zone: An attraction towards reserved, scholarly or selfish people

- Venus Zone: An attraction towards artists, celebrities or theatrical people

- Mercury Zone: An attraction towards persuasive or business people

Branches from the Saturn Line

Career Direction
A: Leadership or bossiness
B: Art, music, beauty, creativity
C: Business, trading, teaching, sales

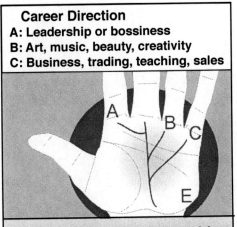

Branches from the Saturn Line

The Saturn Line shows changes and developments in career on the outer hand, and satisfaction with life direction on the inner hand. This line shows social involvement and social integration. Although career is an obvious and very important form of social integration, supportive roles in family such as motherhood and other supportive community roles should be included.

A branch terminating on the:

- Jupiter Zone shows leadership or bossiness.
- Venus Zone suggests artistic endeavours or involvement in some artistic community.

- Mercury Zone, which is frequently called the 'Mercury Line,' records career choices in the field of communication or business, which might include teaching or sales.

Combining with hand types

When considering the meaning of any branch from a main line, it is important to remember to take into account the type of hand on which this line is found.

For example, if the hand type is earthy (broad and muscular with few lines) then this line shows a preference for industry and some business ability.

If a branch from the Saturn Line terminating on the Mercury Zone is found on the sensitive emotional hand (soft supple and slender) it indicates intuition and sensitive emotional expression.

The same line found on the intellectual communicator's hand (long flat hard palm and bony fingers) would suggest sales ability and persuasiveness.

Questions to Test Your Understanding
(see Page 155 for answers)

Are the following statements true or false?

1: A branch from the Life Line to the Venus zone shows enthusiasm for art.
2: A branch from the Head Line to the Mercury zone shows thinking about art.
3: A branch from the Saturn Line to the Jupiter zone shows leadership or bossiness.
4. A branch from the Heart Line to the Venus zone shows attraction towards business people.
5. A branch from the Head Line to the Jupiter Zone shows 'bigness of thought' and ambitious ideas.

Lesson 25

Secondary Lines

The secondary lines are secondary to the main story. While each has its own definite meaning, its interpretation must include the 'big picture' shown by the major lines and the overall hand shape. A more 'major' secondary line, included by some authors in the category of the main lines is the Mercury Line which runs from the lower palm towards the Mercury finger.

A: The Venus Line

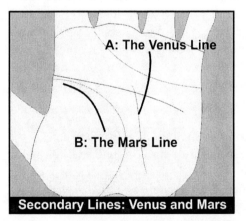

Secondary Lines: Venus and Mars

This line is usually called 'Sun Line' or 'Apollo Line' in the literature. As with the Venus Finger, this line, which is so much associated with art and creativity, will be called the 'Venus Line'. It shows artistry, talent, skill, creative expression, and pleasure in general. It is important to match this line with the hand structure. For example, on a long bony hand with square fingertips this line cannot show creativity as there is little creative energy present. Rather it shows some talent or skill of a technical nature, or perhaps skill at oratory.

When the Venus line is long and deep it suggests special talent, especially if creative energies are shown elsewhere on the hands. A common combination is the Saturn line stopping at the Heart Line and the Venus line beginning at the Heart Line. This combination frequently records divorce followed by a more fulfilling life afterwards, with perhaps an acceptance of less financial reward. By itself the Venus Line beginning from the Heart Line suggests fulfillment after the mid-forties. If the Venus Line is a branch from the Saturn Line it suggests a career or enterprise associated with the arts.

A Venus line which begins low on the palm is more indicative of the serious career artist or artisan.

B: The Mars Line

This line has its energy source in the Outer Mars Zone and swings down between the thumb and the Life Line towards the wrist area. It can be long or short but generally is at least one inch long. It shows a strong fighting spirit. If the Outer Mars Zone and the Sun Mount are well developed then this line indicates an endowment of feisty energy. This line acts like an extra energy reserve in times of difficulty. In Indian palmistry this line is said to show a supportive person.

In the negative it can show reactivity and defensiveness, and sometimes inappropriate aggression. Again the hand shape will guide your assessment. On a fragile or weak hand with a short Jupiter finger there will be less inclination towards assertive expression, and therefore the Mars Line will record defensiveness. On a thick powerful firm hand with a short Jupiter finger it will amplify stamina and stubbornness and passive resistance to unwanted demands.

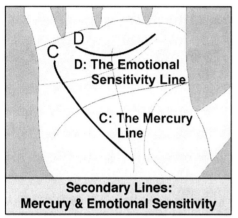

Secondary Lines:
Mercury & Emotional Sensitivity

C: The Mercury Line

The name of this line describes its termination: the Mercury zone. It can originate from deep within the palm, from the Saturn line, or from the Mount of the Moon. Its beginning from the Saturn line suggests a career directed towards communication of some type.

Note that Mercury rules exchange and therefore business and industry, and therefore a well marked Mercury line can indicate a career choice in one of these areas. Match the line with the hand type. On a more sophisticated hand it may indicate an aptitude for sales or business. On an intellectual hand (knotty fingers, long palm and fingers, inflexible) the Mercury line shows persuasive skills when combined with a strong head line. On a very earthy (thick, broad, muscular, few lines), this line shows industry and sometimes the buying and selling of goods.

If this line is ladder-like it suggests digestive problems. If this line is absent it is an indication of robust health, as long as there are no contrary indications found elsewhere on the hand (always check the Life Line for questions on health). If this line is deeply marked it shows a very active nervous system and good communication skills. If this line has its source on the Mount of the Moon it indicates a strong intuitive or creative response to life's challenges.

D: The Emotional Sensitivity Line (the Girdle of Venus)

This line, which is often called 'the Girdle of Venus', links the two sides of the palm which represent the inner and outer worlds, showing a need to find deep meaning and express inner tensions. The presence of this line can indicate prenatal tension, showing that the mother was stressed while pregnant. Prenatal stress can sensitise the unborn child and create a need to reach out for a deeper meaning or connection with others in later life. Sometimes this search for inner meaning finds expression in the occult, psychology, art, or spiritual interests.

The presence of this line normally shows sensitivity to alcohol and drugs. When this line is broken into many pieces in can indicate neurosis.

However this line is common on the sensitive emotional hand (soft slender and supple) and therefore it is less remarkable on this hand type as emotional sensitivity and reactivity is to be expected. Compare this to its placement on earthy muscular hands (broad and muscular with few lines). Its presence on these hands is most unusual. This line is out of place on the earth hand and indicates someone who has an unusual outlet for expressing their inner tensions or who has a problem with drugs or alcohol. While perhaps unremarkable on the emotional sensitive hand, its presence on earthy muscular hands is remarkable, and its meaning should be explored within the context of the client's lifestyle.

I do not call this line the Girdle of Venus because this name was given to the line in Victorian times and carried the meaning of nymphomania, which I believe is incorrect. Yes its presence does record a heightened sensitivity, and perhaps the need to make a connection with others might result in promiscuity, but this is something I have never verified. Therefore I think to use this word might be insulting if per chance the client was aware of its original meaning. It does record heightened emotional sensitivity and acts like a second Heart Line, amplifying emotional responses.

F-J: The Relationship and Children Lines

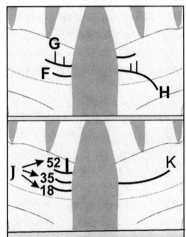

F: Marriage Line
G: Childrens Line
H: Divorce Line
I: Timing Guesstimate
J: Timing
K: Fantasy/Pleasure Line
Secondary Lines
Marriage & Children

So many women ask about these lines and want to know how many marriages and children they will have. Unfortunately these lines are not very reliable as they are easily confused with stress lines. In my experience of reading hands these lines are not a reliable indicator of either marriage or children. However most clients expect them to be an indication of marriage and children and are disappointed when told otherwise.

Horizontal lines (F) are said to show marriage or a committed relationship, and vertical lines (G) linked to these horizontal lines are said to show children. The strong vertical lines which are connected to the horizontal marriage lines are said in the old literature to indicate boys and the weaker vertical lines are said to indicate girls! In today's world such a statement is very politically incorrect. I have not been able to validate this theory.

The horizontal lines often do correlate with marriages or serious relationships, but there examples of people who have had only one lifetime partner with many lines. This brings into question the nature of this line. Some say that these lines correspond to times of heightened sexual need which would show different stages within a secure marriage, or different lovers, or different partners for those who have different partners at various stages in life. The discussion of sexuality with a client is such a sensitive subject that it is difficult to validate any hypothesis. Few people want to reveal all! The cultural norms that exist within an individual's life and society will influence the interpretation of these lines.

What I have validated to my own satisfaction is the so called 'divorce line' (H). This is a horizontal line that curves downward, crossing the Heart Line before fading. It usually indicates the demise of a serious relationship, which may or may not be a marriage. The hands do not record a piece of paper to show marriage as such, but merely the experience of a relationship.

The dating of these lines (I) is always a guesstimate. We begin at the Heart Line and finish at the base of the Mercury finger. However the beginning point at the Heart Line is unlikely to be zero as most people do not have romantic relationships until their teens or later, and in most cases people do not begin serious relationships after their 70's – and yes there are exceptions.

I find that a line beginning about midway between the Heart Line and the base of the Mercury finger is about 35. The timing lines at 'I' in the diagram on the previous page show timing dates above and below this. With such a small space available to indicate timing your best efforts will only ever be a 'guesstimate'. Double-checking with the Heart Line can improve this. For example if the Heart Line is very long, beginning on the Jupiter zone, showing that the client fell in love at an early age, then the lowest line will indicate an earlier beginning. Conversely if the Heart Line has its beginning under the Saturn finger then we can assume that the timing of the marriage lines can be taken from a later time in life.

If there are significant breaks in the Heart Line at a similar time on both hands, check with your client as to whether this correlated with some romantic breakup and the age at which it occurred. This timing may assist with dating the marriage lines. My suggestion is that you only ever provide 'guesstimates' for future events. If the client has a history of breakups then it might be more important to ascertain why this is happening, and if some strategy or therapy can be place in place to minimise romantic problems in the future.

A very long 'marriage' line (J) can indicate a powerful emphasis on pleasure and fantasy.

K: The 'Therapist's Line' (Ring of Solomon)

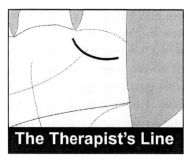
The Therapist's Line

This line which is traditionally called the 'Ring of Solomon', links the wisdom contained in the Saturn Zone with outer world and other people, which is represented by the empty space between the Thumb and Jupiter Finger. It is sometimes partially formed and is relatively common. The actual ability to counsel others will be shown by other indications. On hands where the lines are an absolute mess there is little ability to offer appropriate counsel to others, and a different occupation should be encouraged.

The old books say that this line indicates a love of hidden wisdom. Its presence on the Jupiter zone can in the negative amplify pride and the desire to appear superior. If it completely encircles the Jupiter finger it effectively cuts off the energies to this finger, which may manifest in self esteem issues. There are divergent opinions in the literature as to whether the presence of this line is a positive or negative marking.

Questions to Test Your Understanding
(see Page 155 for answers)

Are the following statements true or false?

1: The Mars Line shows ambition.

2: The Mercury Line shows an aptitude for communication.

3: The Venus Line is often called the 'Sun Line' in traditional literature.

4. The Emotional Sensitivity Line has special importance when found on earth or elementary hands.

5. The horizontal lines between the base of the Mercury finger and the Heart Line show children.

Lesson 26

Incidental Marks and Signs

The Grille

Indicates obstacles against the success of the positive qualities indicted by the mount or zone on which it is found. This formation of lines criss-crossing each other suggest that the energy is moving at cross-purposes, which aggravates the underlying energy and has a negative interpretation.

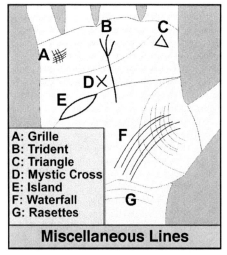

A: Grille
B: Trident
C: Triangle
D: Mystic Cross
E: Island
F: Waterfall
G: Rasettes

Miscellaneous Lines

Jupiter: Egotism, pride, dominating others, issues with self esteem.

Saturn: Misfortune, melancholy nature and morbid tendencies, guilt.*

Venus: Vanity, folly, desire for celebrity.

Mercury: Instability, nervousness, unprincipled persuasion.

Luna: Restlessness, discontent, disquiet, vague anxieties.

Sun: A grille or criss-cross of vertical and horizontal lines is normal on the Sun Mount. The vertical lines represent the lymphatic system and the horizontal lines represent the glandular system. When the horizontal lines cross the Life Line and dip down towards the lower palm like a waterfall, glandular stress or fever is sometimes indicated.

The Triangle

Indicates success associated with the qualities of the mount or zone on which it is found.

The triangle is always positive.

Jupiter: More than the usual success in the management of people and organising everyday affairs.

Saturn: Talent and inclination for mystical work, for delving into the occult.

Venus: Practical application of art, and a calm demeanour towards success and fame-never spoilt by celebrity.

Mercury: Checks restless qualities. Success in business or financial dealings.

Inner or Outer Mars: Science in warfare. Great calmness in crisis. Presence of mind in danger.

Luna: Scientific method in following out the ideas of the imagination.

Upstanding Trident or Branching Tree

Excellent sign of success in any area - generally found at the top of the Saturn Line or Venus Line.

Mystic Cross

Found between the Head and Heart Lines. Traditionally said to indicate mysticism, occultism and superstition, and shows a natural interest in spiritual matters. Legend has it that the Mystic Cross was a necessary mark for entry into mystic orders of the pre-Christian era.

High towards Jupiter Finger suggests a belief in mysticism for one's own life. Such people want their fortunes told and are motivated more by curiosity to know how their ambitions will turn out than by a deeper interest into the study involved for its own sake.

Closer to the Heart Line than the Head Line: Superstitious nature.

Over the centre of the Head Line when it takes a sharp curve downward: Highly superstitious nature – especially when the Head Line is very short.

Independent from the Head Line: Greatest potential for occultism.

Touching the Saturn Line: Love of mysticism will influence career.

Islands

Islands always indicate problems, and are generally associated with repressed hurt and trauma.

Following are some brief interpretations. On a line coming from the:

Sun Mount to the Heart Line: A romantic interest influence brings trouble and disgrace.

Sun Mount to the Head Line: A bad influence will direct talents and intentions into a direction that brings failure and disgrace.

Sun Mount to the Saturn Line: Bad influence will affect career and progress according to how the line proceeds after the influence. Influence will be felt at the time that the line touches the Fate Line.

Below are interpretations of islands on the zones of the palm:

Jupiter: Weakens pride and ambition.

Saturn: Misfortune. Melancholy.

Venus: Weakens natural talents, sometimes indicating disgrace.

Mercury: Instability. Nervousness. Too changeable to really succeed in business or science.

Inner or Outer Mars: Weak spirit. Cowardice.

Circles

I have never seen this mark except as a scar.

Only favourable on the Venus Zone.

Touching any major line: Person will have difficulty clearing themselves of misfortune - will go around and around in circles and not be able to break free.

Spot

Generally a sign of temporary illness.*Bright red spot on Head Line: Shock or injury to head from blow or fall. *Black or blue: Nervous illness. *Bright red on Mercury Line: Fever. *Bright red on Life Line: Feverish illness.

Rascettes

The Indian palmists suggest that these lines show health welath and long life. I have not been able to validate this.

However when the upper rascette closest to the palm is broken and protrudes a little into the palm it is said to show difficulty with childbirth. I have had this verified on many occasion but have not seen it validated by any scientific test.

Questions to Test Your Understanding
(see Page 155 for answers)

Are the following statements true or false?
1: A grille marking on the Sun mount shows bad health.
2: Triangles are always a positive sign.
3: The mystic cross is usually found on the Sun mount.
4. A triangle on the Venus zone shows that success and fame is not spoilt by celebrity.

Section 4

HAND TYPES

Lesson 27

Hand Types

The most important part of any study of the hands is the shape. It is the primary foundation of interpretation.

Over the years a number of models have been proposed to describe and classify hand shapes, with each description focused on a particular aspect of the hands.

In the 1850's a Frenchman named Desbarolles wrote "Les Mysteres de la Main" in which he categorised seven types, based mainly upon their finger tip type. These seven types are the elementary, square, philosophic, conic, psychic, spatulate and mixed. This system was also used by Cheiro and many other authors.

In the 1960's Noel Jaquin proposed 4 types, based upon a combination of palm and finger length: Practical (methodical and realistic), Intellectual (thoughtful and systematic), Intuitive (emotional and responsive) and Sensitive (caring and imaginative).

These four shapes correspond to those shapes based on the astrological elements: earth, air, fire and water.

A third typology was proposed by Dr. Charlotte Wolff (1897-1986) in her books "The Human Hand" and "The Hand in Psychological Diagnosis" and was based on the endocrine system:

TYPE	ELEMENTARY	PRACTICAL	FIRE	AIR	PHILOSOPHICAL	WATER	SMALL
DESCRIPTION	Elementary Basic Outdoors	Physical Outgoing Outdoors	Intuitive Active	Thoughtful Practical Organiser	Intellectual Technical Persuasive	Sensitive Emotional	Sensitive BIG ideas Lively
PALM WIDTH	Wide	Wide	Long	Wide	Long	Long	Long
FINGER LENGTH	Short	Short	Short	Long	Long	Long	Medium
FINGER TIPS	Round Square	Square Spatulate	Round Conic	Round Square	Round	Conic Pointed	Conic
FINGER SMOOTHNESS	Smooth	Smooth KNOTTY	Smooth	Knotty	Knotty	Smooth	Smooth
PADDING	Padded	Padded	Padded	Medium Padding	Flat	Padded Flat	Padded Flat
HARDNESS	Hard	Hard	Soft	Hard	Hard	Soft	Soft
FLEXIBILITY	Inflexible	Inflexible	Flexible	Inflexible	Inflexible	Flexible	Flexible
LINES	Few	Few - Medium	Medium Numerous	Medium	Medium - Many	Numerous	Numerous

HAND CLASSIFICATION ACCORDING TO SHAPE

Elementary simple (basic and simple personality)

Elementary irregular (basic with unusual tendencies)

Motoric fleshy (social and outgoing)

Motoric bony (thoughtful two-sided personality)

Sensitive small (intellectual and childlike)

Sensitive long (emotionally sensitive)

In this typology the elementary and motoric types are classified as prehensile (enjoying purposeful action) and tactile (expressive).

A fourth system has been proposed by William G. Benham in his "Laws of Scientific Hand Reading" in 1946 which is based on the padded mounts on the palm. These seven types which follow the names of the seven traditional planets are: Saturn, Jupiter, Mars, Sun (Apollonian), Venus, Mercury and the Moon.

Benham claims that this typology is superior to the others because it reveals the nature of the human subject in its entirety, instead of simply identifying a few qualities.

Successful hand reading is the art of combination. The hand reader who is able to correctly categorise hands has a major advantage because categories offer a comprehensive personality description, although some classification types are more comprehensive than others. It is like a 'package deal'. If you can identify the package you will know what is inside without needing to analyse each aspect of the hands. The further advantage is that by identifying which part of the hand is 'out of character' then it is possible to quickly identify the source of difficulties that the client might be experiencing.

Example 1: An elementary hand has the 'emotional sensitive' line (Girdle of Venus), then this person will have an unusual need to find some deep connection with life, or perhaps fall into some form of chemical addiction. This line will draw them away from the normally satisfying rural and simple lifestyle that is enjoyed by people with elementary hands.

Example 2: A client has emotional sensitive hands with an unusually long thumb and Jupiter finger. This emotional sensitive type is naturally more nurturing and receptive, but the overlong Jupiter finger and thumb would draw them into positions of leadership, which is a natural contradiction. If you know the hand type the most unusual feature on the hands is likely to be the main contributor to the problems about which the client has come to consult you.

The system of hand classification that I use is a combination of Jaquin's system with a number of adaptations inspired by Wolff. Most astrologers are familiar with the four elemental shapes: fire, earth, air and water. Add to these classifications the variables of hardness and flexibility and we can define these shapes more correctly.

Most hands show a dominance of one type, or a combination of two types.

A simple guide

If a hand has knuckled fingers, then there is a strong intellectual component to that personality.

If the hands are soft and supple, then there is a strong emotional component.

If the hands are thick and coarse, then there is a strong preference for physical activity and the outdoors.

Detailed hand types with personality descriptions

The Elementary Hand
Description
This hand has a heavy and thick appearance, and is strong, rigid and hard, with smooth sausage like fingers, with round – square tips. There are very few lines, usually just the Life Line, Head Line and Heart Line. The Life Line must be strong and well formed for a competent and fufiling life. The hands are rough and coarse. There is no refinement. The fingers are medium to short, and the palms usually broad or large.

Interpretation
This is a basic and solid individual, non-demonstrative, stodgy and reliable. Positive characteristics are trustworthiness and loyalty, plus the ability to work hard. Their stiff fingers show fixed ideas and stubbornness, and the overall shape shows limited social responses.

These are 'earthy' people who love the outdoors. Their lives are uninteresting by more sophisticated standards. They love routine and in relationship have set roles and routines. Food, shelter and sex are their main requirements in life. They have no time for books or intellectual theories. They like the isolation of nature and can get very stressed in a city environment.

Manual labour or farming or some type of subsistance from the land is most suited to those with elementary hands. The lives of those with elementary hands are cyclical, in tune with the rhythms of nature. These are instinctive people who have a natural response to animals and are best suited to a rural environment.

If they present at a consultation you can be sure that some serious upset has overtaken them. Suggesting anything remotely intellectual is a waste of time. You need to offer practical answers or refer them to someone who can provide assistance.

If the fingers are more flexible or the lines more numerous more elasticity and sociability would be evident.

The Practical Hand

Description

Again the hand is thick broad and strong, and muscular and firm. They are usually well padded. These hands are inflexible. However the fingers, which are usually medium length, show more differentiation than the elementary hand. The finger tips can be round to square. There are more lines than on the elementary hand but they are not numerous, although there is normally a Saturn line.

Interpretation

These are outgoing people who love company and social activities. They can often be found in community and sporting functions, enjoying a level of involvement that provides some camaraderie. Emotionally they are non-responsive, tending to bottle up the feelings. This is natural and needs to be respected. The inflexibility of the hands indicates emotional inertia - these people who do not easily express their emotions, and have difficulty doing so when this expression is needed. The emotions run in steady cycles, and tend to get bottled up. Emotional release is often found in music, especially singing and the piano. Although they are outgoing in the sense of wanting to join together in social activities, they can be shy and non-assertive. Those with a longer Jupiter finger make excellent leaders and are found running many community organisations and businesses. They have a strong need for exercise and sex, and if their job keeps them indoors they will need a lot of exercise.

They are good at solving practical and mechanical problems, and can be found in those professions where practical skills are required. If the finger tips are square they will appreciate working in an environment where there are clear rules and established methods.

The broad firm palm shows a practical, outgoing and hardworking nature. The well padded palm shows a strong need for social interaction. This is the hand of the friendly person. Emotional fulfilment largely depends on their ability to interact socially and find some form of community acceptance.

The broad palms indicate practical purposeful activity - practical accomplishment brings satisfaction.

These people are noted for their energy and persistence, sense of justice, and the need to work to some agreed rules or principles of living. Rules offer a sense of stability, and channel their powerful drives into constructive activity, ensuring that their animal instincts do not run wild and destroy their accomplishments.

These people are steady and reliable. They enjoy pleasant social activities. Because of their ability to deal with people and their practical nature they are often found in positions of management, whether in business or in positions of community responsibility.

Some Variations

When the knuckles of the fingers are prominent, there is a strong logical and analytical ability, giving balance between thinking and feeling.

Short fingers indicate impatience, as well as a greater capacity to grasp the overall picture. This is the more intuitive hand.

A hand with very few lines shows someone who is close to mother earth. The more lines and the finer the skin, then the more likely the person is to take on big projects requiring involving the co-operation of others.

This hand type is similar to the thoughtful air hand but more practical, more 'hands on', more intuitive (if the fingers are smooth), less theoretical.

The Thoughtful—Air hand

Description

Broad palm, long fingers, usually knotty, with square to round tips. Inflexible hands. Moderate padding.

Interpretation

The main difference between this and the Practical Earth Hand is that the fingers are longer (showing more thoughtfulness), and other features of the hand, such as skin texture and line markings, show greater refinement and social awareness.

This person places a lot of emphasis upon understanding and the need to make sense of things. This person enjoys communicating this understanding in a methodical way. There is more precision and love of detail. This person loves to deal with the external world outside of self, and is often found in organisational or administrative positions. If the hands are relatively flat the personality is more withdrawn with a reliance on technical expertise to find an acceptance in a social role and place in the community. If the hands are well padded, then this person is more socially oriented.

The knotty fingers show a love of detail and analysis, and the broad palm provides a practical foundation for all activities.

If the Mercury Finger is long and the Head Line strong and well marked there can be excellent sales and persuasive skills. If the palm is well padded these persuasive skills will be directed with warmth and feeling.

Similar to the philosopher's hand but more practical, less theoretical, more able to connect with people's feelings, more extroverted, less tendency towards escapism, less articulate and skillful.

The Philosopher's hand (The Intellectual Hand)

Description

Flat narrow palms and long knotty fingers. The hands are inflexible and can be rigid. The finger tips are often square or round.

Interpretation

The flatness of the hand shows that the mind rules over the emotions, the long palm shows the need for expression, the knotty fingers show the detailed analytical approach, and the rigidity of the hand indicates locked in emotions. There are usually more lines than on the Thoughtful Air Hand, but sometimes they have a hesitant look.

Altogether this is a personality needing to express itself through the mind. There is a strong need for emotional release, with mental expression and physical activity being the only outlets available.

The long palm and knotty fingers suggest an introverted person with an excellent mind and capacity for communication. In spite of their inner isolation, these people have charm and persuasive power that commands attention.

Life is like a seesaw... these intellectual communicators need to be with people one moment, and then need to be away from them; they enjoy city life for the mental stimulation it offers, but need the wide open spaces to withdraw and deal with their emotions. They excel at the skilful use of words and communication of ideas, and prefer symbolism in art. They make fantastic salespeople. They can be meticulous and pedantic.

Their intelligence is abstract, with the ego centred in the mind. Because a sense of self worth is derived from using the brain, accumulation of knowledge in some specialist area is important. Technical know-how is often their strength. Logical deduction comes easy. These thoughtful communicators have a very reasonable approach to life, but without the emotion to back it up.

Their strength is in their ability to learn skilful techniques, mechanical and technical skills are favourites. They make excellent salespeople, able to learn and apply proven techniques without difficulty. They are also often found in trades because of their technical expertise.

Their biggest weakness is inner isolation and loneliness. They desperately need people, but pull back from emotional contact. They are cut off from the feelings and live in the mind. There is awkwardness with cuddles and physical caress. At their worst they are empty egotists, skilfully manipulating others with the charm of their words and reasoning capacity, with no real feeling or concern for those they deal with.

On the other hand, the more evolved kind has forged a close relationship between the mind and the inner feelings, with the ability to link the inner and outer worlds and so achieve a lasting inner harmony. The lines on the palm will show the extent of feeling and the ability to relate this to others.

Variations

Fine skin texture will show the professional communicator who likes to use the mind. These people often have an aptitude for working with computers. Coarse skin shows a leaning towards the skilled trades and outdoor work.

Pointed and conic finger tips soften the hard logical approach of this person, adding imagination and dreaminess to a well developed mind.

This hand type is similar to the thoughtful air hand but more theoretical, more introspective, more articulate and skilful, more awkward with relating to others, and has a greater need for privacy.

The Intuitive Hand - Fire hand

Description
Long palm and short fingers. The palms are usually padded, the lines numerous, and the skin texture medium to fine.

Interpretation

The long palm reveals a more emotional nature where the inner world is what motivates this person to action. This short fingers (relative to the palm) show quickness of thought and action. This person is intuitive, fiery and expressive. We may also describe this person as enthusiastic, impatient, exciting, changeable, active and warm (especially if the hands are well padded).

There is so much variety in the flexibility and firmness of this hand shape that it is more difficult to offer a comprehensive personality overview. When the hands are firm and thick there can be powerful resolve and explosive energy. If the skin is coarse this can manifest in a love of powerful machines such as motorbikes, engines and motor vehicles.

If the hands are relatively inflexible and more firm then the personality has more resolve and these people will often take charge if the Jupiter finger shows sufficient length.

If the hands are softer and more flexible then there is a strong similarity with the sensitive emotional water hand, but with much more spontaneity and less tendency to be introspective.

The Sensitive Emotional Hand - Water Hand

Description

The hands are slender, soft and supple with long smooth fingers and fine skin. The lines are fine and numerous and often broken.

Interpretation

This is a very emotional person, sensitive and imaginative. This person needs to feel things. If the hand shows sufficient padding, then this person can be supportive and nurturing. These people love to dream about love and romance.

When the hands are thin and flat, there are more escapist tendencies, with a preference live in a more dreamy and introspective world.

The softness and suppleness of the hands permits the easy flow of emotion and responsiveness to others. The long palm shows that the primary need is to express feelings, and the long fingers show that this expression is thorough and detailed. The fine skin indicates a deep appreciation of beauty and refinement, a distaste for coarseness and vulgarity, and need for refinement and beauty in their surroundings.

These people feel deeply, and are very good at attending the needs of others. They are excellent nurturers with a strong ability to recognise the emotional needs of others.

Intimacy is the strongest need of this person. They need, above all, to express their deepest feelings and share them with another. Their romantic fantasies usually emphasise emotional closeness.

These people can be deeply moved by the smallest thing, and take things very personally. A little praise and lots of cuddles take them to nirvana! Love is the nutrient on which they subsist. They will also notice its absence very quickly.

Imagination is very strong in the sensitive emotional types. They are soulful dreamers. Family life and the quality of the relationship is extremely important to these people. The lines on the palm will reflect their happiness in these vital areas, and in particular will indicate the quality of intimacy in their life.

Variations

Variations

If the hands are particularly weak (particularly flexible or soft, short or very supple thumbs), then there is little practicality and overwhelming emotion. Unless the hands show unusual strength, such as a very strong thumb combined with a straight head line, then there will be little aptitude for business.

Fine skin always indicates fine thoughts and a finely balanced nervous system. Emotional stress is what will unbalance these people. If the hands are particularly supple, then low blood pressure may be indicated.

Coarser skin texture shows a greater aptitude for dealing with the practicalities of life, and a stronger preference for physical activities. However this is a contradiction in type and not often found.

The Sensitive Small Hand

Description

This hand is small in comparison to most hands, often narrow and more often found in women than men. It is usually very flexible. The outer side of the hand (the Mercury finger side of the hand) can be long and well developed, showing powerful emotions and imagination. The palm is more often long and the fingers short, showing a strong similarity with the intuitive fire hand, but smaller, more flexible and more refined. The fingers are usually conical.

Interpretation

People with this hand type show a preference for the indoors and private social groups where there is intimacy and security in togetherness.

The lines are numerous showing a nervous disposition which will be reflected in lifestyle. The fingers are usually conical showing a dreamy and imaginative approach to life. Square thumbs on this type are a contradiction, as they show a more mechanical approach on a hand which shows a disposition to elasticity and imagination. The thumb is very flexible, showing versatility and the capacity to learn from others. A stiff thumb on this hand type would add more practicality and a need for security.

These people love the big picture and like to do things quickly. They are excitable, sometimes brilliant, and hyper-sensitive. They are dramatists and have little resistance to life's challenges. Their responses to life are reactive rather than reasoned. If the thumb is strong and the Head Line is even then there is more control.

People with 'sensitive small' hands live on an emotional roller coaster with big ups and downs, living a childlike existence, and not particularly stable. Their thinking is big and intuitive. They grasp ideas quickly and turn them to their advantage. They are usually articulate and often histrionic. Their numerous lines add variety to expression. If they are too numerous the expression becomes hysterical, neurotic and attention seeking, especially if the emotional sensitive line (Girdle of Venus) is present.

By nature the sensitive small personality does not possess physical dynamism, so a strong Life Line is always a plus. If also it is red then overindulgence is present. If the Jupiter finger is bent toward the Saturn finger there is a defensive reaction to the realities of life, which limits an otherwise adaptable personality.

If the person with the sensitive small hands is partnered and loved by someone with practical and well padded hands, then a stable lifestyle can result.

Questions to Test Your Understanding
(see Page 156 for answers)

Are the following statements true or false?

1: The elementary hand shows mental agility.

2: Long flat hands with knotty fingers show an outgoing personality.

3: Sensitive small hands show lively people whose energy fluctuates.

4. People with Sensitive Long hands are very good at business.

5. People with the Philosopher's hands alternate between wanting company and needing privacy.

6. People with fire shaped hands love to take time and deliberate over matters.

Section 5
The Genetic Engravings

Lesson 28

Finger Prints and Palm Prints

The skin ridge patterns on the fingers and palms reveal the genetic inheritance. These patterns are found all over the palm and fingers. Under microscopic analysis they appear as furrows, looking very similar to sand dunes.

Of particular interest are the tri-radii (small triangles). These are the power points from which the 3 skin ridges radiate in different directions.

It should be noted that the patterns revealed by the fingerprints and the dermatoglyphics on the palm show the underlying psychological structure - a structure that does not change with age. This structure should always be combined with hand shape and major hand features to give a clear picture of the underlying background context into which all other features should be read.

On the finger tips these tri-radii determine the shape of the fingerprints. These fingerprint formations reveal the way thoughts and feelings are processed by the mind, as well as the way observations from the outside world are assimilated.

Below each of the fingers there is normally a tri-radius. These are the power points indicating the focus of energy for each of the finger zones (often mistakenly called mounts). From these tri-radii are energy lines called radials. These radials demarcate the underlying energy fields of the palm.

The whorl fingerprint must have 2 tri-radii to be a whorl - if there is only one then it is in all probability a loop. These tri-radii are found at the base of the whorl. The composite loop (sometimes called the double loop) must also have 2 tri-radii.

Both the ulna and radial loops have only one tri-radius. The arch and tented arch fingerprints have no tri-radii.

On the palm itself these points reveal the concentration of energy fields. These power points have a direct connection with the actual content and supply of available energy as revealed by the mounts and lines of the palm.

The placement of the tri-radii on the upper palm beneath the fingers, in relation to the fingers, indicates how that energy is expressed.

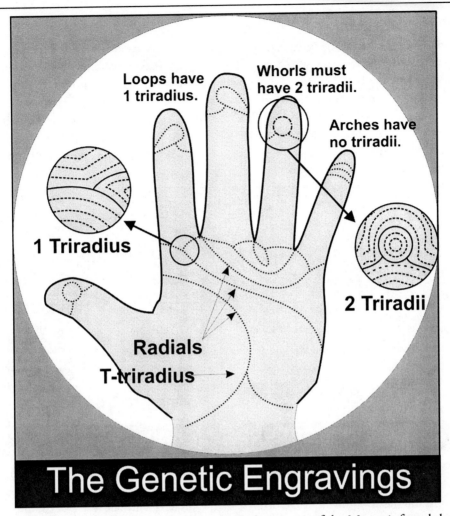

Loops have
1 triradius.

Whorls must
have 2 triradii.

Arches have
no triradii.

1 Triradius

2 Triradii

Radials

T-triradius

The Genetic Engravings

At the base of the hand, normally towards the Mount of the Moon, is found the major power point usually referred to as the "T-tri-radius".

However when this tri-radius is displaced further towards the Mount of the Moon, it gives more space for the conscious and physical side of the personality is to be expressed.

When this power point hugs the outer side of the palm near the thumb, social outgoing attitudes are reduced, accompanied by a strong desire for a sense of roots and a sense of belonging. Outgoing social attitudes are reduced, resulting in more self directed and introspective activities. In this case the lunar energies are allowed greater scope, adding anxiety and introversion on a hand with many negative markings, and mysticism and intuition on a strong hand.

A very high T-triradius is found in a higher proportion of people with congenital heart problems, and is also associated with mongolism and other genetic disorders.

The study of the dermatoglyphics on the palm is complex and beyond the scope of this book. In this book the focus is on the fingerprints, which provide a genetic and therefore fundamental influence upon mental attitudes and the processing of psychological and deep seated responses.

The Fingerprints

The underlying genetic blueprint is revealed by the skin ridge patterns we call fingerprints. The fingerprints reveal the way thoughts and feelings are processed by the brain. So in order to understand the way the brain processes thoughts and feelings which have moved up through the hand these patterns must be examined. In this examination it is the overall pattern of the fingerprints which is assessed. Small deviations and variations are disregarded. While the police and othere protective services use fingerprints for identification purposes and are therefore focused upon minute variations, this is not the concern of the hand analyst. It is the overall appearance of the fingerprints that is important.

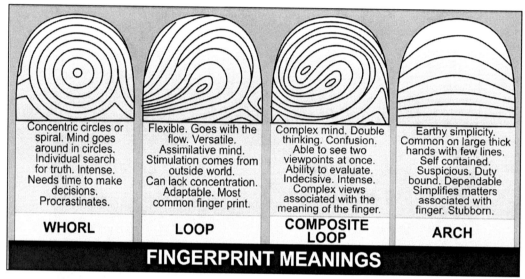

WHORL	LOOP	COMPOSITE LOOP	ARCH
Concentric circles or spiral. Mind goes around in circles. Individual search for truth. Intense. Needs time to make decisions. Procrastinates.	Flexible. Goes with the flow. Versatile. Assimilative mind. Stimulation comes from outside world. Can lack concentration. Adaptable. Most common finger print.	Complex mind. Double thinking. Confusion. Able to see two viewpoints at once. Ability to evaluate. Indecisive. Intense. Complex views associated with the meaning of the finger.	Earthy simplicity. Common on large thick hands with few lines. Self contained. Suspicious. Duty bound. Dependable Simplifies matters associated with finger. Stubborn.

FINGERPRINT MEANINGS

The fingerprints should be included in the study of the structure of the hands. They never change. Primarily they reflect mental attitudes. There full interpretation comes from combining the meaning of the fingerprint with the finger on which it is placed, and all this within the context of the hand type.

There are 4 types of fingerprints:

1. The loop, which has 2 variations: the ulnar loop and the radial loop.
2. The composite loop.
3. The whorl.
4. The arch, which has 2 variations: the low arch and the tented arch.

The loop

The loop curls in from the side of the finger like a lasso.

The ulnar loop

The ulnar loop opens from the ulna (Mercury finger) side of the palm. The loop is the most common fingerprint, found on 64% of all fingers across the globe. It reveals an adaptable response to life and a flexible expression.

The loop shows that thoughts and feelings are processed by the brain in an easy flowing manner. This permits adaptability to life's changing circumstances. There is more variety of responses available, and more receptivity to various stimuli from the outside world.

The radial loop

The radial loop opens from the radial (thumb) side of the hand. This pattern is most common on the Jupiter finger, and reveals self-determination and a need for independent choice. A certain adaptability is still present, but with a need for self expression. This print is less common on the Saturn and Venus fingers and very rare on the Mercury finger.

The composite loop

This loop is actually two loops entwined together. It reveals a natural duality and a complex and intense expression. Double thinking – thinking of two things at once is a dominant characteristic. However the advantage is that this pattern gives the ability to evaluate different options and see different points of view simultaneously.

In the negative it shows confusion and muddled thinking.

The whorl

The whorl consists of either a series of concentric circles or a spiral. Its shape reveals an intensity of expression. The thinking process goes around and around in circles. People with a lot of these prints go over an idea many times before arriving at a conclusion.

This type of fingerprint acts like a spring. They are slow to wind up, hence the reputation for procrastination, and intense when released.

People with many whorls are very intense and focused. Look to what features dominate the rest of the hands to understand what aspects of the personality are being amplified.

People with many whorls are seekers after the truth. Whorls will intensify the expression of other hand features. On a complex hand they can amplify the complexity to the disadvantage of the client. Many whorls will always show a strong focus. The most outstanding and unusual features of the hands will be the beneficiaries, for good or ill.

The arch

This pattern looks like a hill, with layers over layers of sediment. These layers act like a blanket covering the rising energies.

The low arch

The low arch pattern shows self containment, a strong sense of duty, a straight forward person, obstinacy, and a down to earth approach to life's problems. Suspicion is another trait associated with this pattern, especially when there are many arches.

This is a simple pattern which shows an earthy response, and a need for a 'hands-on' approach, such as in the arts, crafts, or mechanics.

Many arches will have a dulling effect on a hand, such as an elementary hand, that is already dull. However on a hand which shows more complex features and a very active mind arches will have a stabilising effect, enabling the client to simplify many of life's complex issues and respond with instinct when presented with intellectual subterfuge.

Arches always show a powerful need to be in nature, which in the city often simply shows the need to be outside, in the weather, particularly when stress begins to build. Exercise outdoors is vital for those who work indoors who have a number of arch fingerprints.

The tented arch

The tented arch is a rare variation of the low arch pattern, with the contours rising to a sharp peak. . This pattern combines the qualities of earthiness with sensitivity and responsiveness, and is often associated with artistic sensitivity. The tented arch fingerprint pattern also adds a quality of innovation, variety and unusualness to the qualities associated with the finger on which it is found.

Combining fingerprint types with fingers

A broad interpretation of the fingerprints on each finger is shown below. To take this further you must distinguish between left and right hands, and the type of hand on which the fingerprint is found.

Loop

Thumb: Adaptability in the will and decision making.

Jupiter: Relaxed and open observation style. Generous attitude to other's point of view.

Saturn: Ethical and moral standards more elastic and adaptable. Can listen to others beliefs.

Venus: Choice in art style and presentation open to change and open to suggestion. Can experiment with different forms of art.

Mercury: Can communicate in a variety of ways, easy to learn new languages. Able to gain financially from understanding the needs of others.

Whorl

Thumb: Intense. Thorough. Strong drive to achieve.

Jupiter: Focused powers of observation. Associated with teaching and science. Dreamer.

Saturn: Ethical and moral standards fixed and certain. Seeks the truth.

Venus: Strong creative energy. Theatrical. The whorl is most commonly found on this finger. The realist in art.

Mercury: Intense communicator. Fixed style. Wants the truth. Sexual intensity.

Double loop

Thumb: Double thinking. Procrastination. Indecisive.

Jupiter: Sees both sides of a point of view. Good for legal practice.

Saturn: Thinks deeply and thoroughly about ethical concerns. Religious confusion.

Venus: Wants to incorporate different viewpoints into creative pursuits.

Mercury: Wants to present both sides. Goes around in circles.

Arch

Thumb: Down-to-earth. Loves nature and the elements. Strong sense of duty. Determined.

Jupiter: Able to simplify complex ideas. Strong sense of duty. Stubbornness.

Saturn: Conservative viewpoint. Likes the land, rural life. Earthy philosophies.

Venus: Earthy tastes in art. Seeks art for financial gain.

Mercury: Expresses clearly and simply.

Questions to Test Your Understanding
(see Page 155 for answers)

Are the following statements true or false?
1: Arch fingerprint patterns reflect a natural affinity with the rhythms of nature.
2: The loop fingerprints are associated with intensity.
3: Composite loop patterns show the potential for confusion.
4. Whorl fingerprints intensify the meaning of the finger on which they are placed.

Section 6
Putting It All Together

Lesson 29

Putting it all together

Basic procedure for analysing the hands.

This chapter deals with the process of analysis in a hand reading. The following chapter deals with the broader structure of a reading, how it is constructed from a psychological and professional-client relationship perspective.

1. When you greet your client it is always a good idea to shake hands. Women do not always do this although it is more common in America. At this point, usually at the front door of your home or office, the client is usually more focused on meeting you and making some sort of an impression and less focused on what their handshake might reveal. Immediately you will know whether the hands are hard or soft, or if the client is trying to make a big impression (vigorous hand shake).

From the moment you meet your client you are presented with many personality indications, spoken and unspoken. These can include why the client is seeking your services, their issues, and if you are very observant, clients will often reveal the answers to their own questions. The client has come to you for assistance and it is important to use whatever clues are provided to assist your client.

2. Look at the way the client holds their hands naturally – are they clenched, hung listless, fidgety, held with a light inward curl of the fingers (normal). All these provide valuable insights into their personality.

3. When you are seated and introductory social etiquette has been observed, ask the client to hold up their hands, back and front, and take note of the expression of the hands.

4. Ask your client if they are right or left handed. Many will make some claim to ambidexterity. This can be true to a limited extent but you still need to know which hand is most dominant.

This is normally the right hand. The right hand is always the default option. If your client is confused ask them which foot they kick a ball with – the hand on the same side of the body will normally be the dominant hand. If still in doubt ask them to cup their hands together loosely and look through the gap between the fingers. Observe whether they favour the right or left eye – the hand on the same side of the body will normally be the dominant hand.

5. Ask your client why they have come and what they would like from the reading. It is important that this question was asked when they originally contacted you, but it is worth repeating.

6. The first step in analysis is to assess the overall shape of the hands, which must include flexibility, and hardness, and overall line structure. Usually the hands will match one or more hand types, with one type dominating. This will provide you with the ability to make an overall personality assessment.

7. Look for any features which stand out or are unusual, such as extra long or extra short fingers, redness, and rigidity. Make sure you have understood the overall outline/shape before you get lost in the detail of the lines.

8. Many beginning palmists feel overwhelmed at the beginning of a reading, particularly when the hands contain many lines. There is no need to explain each line in absolute detail. This would be too time consuming. Many lines show a very active mind and nervous system. Few lines show a more straightforward approach to life and less nervous energy. Keep it simple!

9. Assess the main lines: Life, Head, Heart and Saturn Line. Describe these lines, always keeping in mind how they match the hand shape. The golden rule is to fit the lines to the shape. Check the difference between right and left hands.

10. In your own mind keep going back to the reason the client has come to see you. Many will say they are just curious. This is rarely true and there is usually some important worry. If you are fortunate your client will have been explicit with their reason for consulting you.

11. Check left and right hands. Keep going back from one to the other and noting the differences. The difference between the hands will reveal their adaptations to life challenges and explain their life strategy for meeting their needs.

12. When you have completed your assessment of the main lines check the secondary lines. This may not always be necessary but can yield important information. Check the difference between the right and left hands and keep in mind how all this fits the context of the hand shape. It is the hand shape which reveals the context of the client's life and it is important to understand their world view and speak in a way that the client can understand.

13. There is no need to examine and explain every tiny line. Many of the small lines simply reflect nervous anxiety. Many small lines reveal nervous worry and anxiety.

14. When you feel you have addressed your client's concerns go back to the hand shape and provide a brief summary, explaining what the shape says about their overall personality and how the standout features reveal their uniqueness. Keep it brief and always finish on a positive note.

The above is only intended as a guide. Over time you will develop your own style and go through a routine that suits your personality and produces the best results for your clients.

Lesson 30

The Underlying Structure

The way in which a professional reading is conducted tends to go through distinct stages, some of which are not clearly separated from each other. Although the way the readings of different consultants may vary to some degree, usually depending on the personality of the consultant, most readings tend to follow a similar pattern.

That pattern is described here so that beginners will be able to better prepare for a reading and know what to expect. One of the most frequent problems encountered by beginners and often by more experienced readers is the first stage: the contract. Probably the second major problem encountered is the last stage: winding it all up so that both the reader and the client go away with a feeling of satisfaction.

1. The Contract

It is most important that before your client comes to see you that a clear understanding has been reached about what both parties expect from the consultation. You should know what the client wants from the consultation, and of course there should be clear agreement about your fee.

If these things are not established in advance then problems can easily arise if you find out you have different expectations than those of your client.

I have spoken to many consultants who have expressed frustration and annoyance because of awkward situations that could have easily been avoided if there had been clear communication from the very beginning.

The problem is that sometimes the consultant is so keen to do business because of financial need that these necessities are ignored. This is sometimes a good reason for having an alternative source of income.

There is no point discovering halfway through a reading that your client expects only fortune-telling if making predictions is not something you are comfortable with. *Nor is there much joy for your client in discovering that your fee is twice what they expected.

If part of your work is to foster clarity and understanding for your client, then it is important that you both begin with clarity and understanding about what you are doing and have a mutual agreement about the fee.

These are the basics upon which your reading is founded.

2. The Preparation of your Environment

a) External:

The setting in which the consultation is to be conducted should be organised so as to establish an environment where you and your client will feel relaxed and uninterrupted.

It is important to add a sense of professionalism if you are serious about your work. This means a neat and clean environment with comfortable seating and amenities close by.

Being constantly interrupted by the phone (buy an answering machine or get your family or secretary to answer it), traffic noise or demanding children (make suitable arrangements for their care) does little in the way of providing the quality time for which your client is paying. Neither do such interruptions assist your clarity of mind or ability to pick up the subtle clues offered by your client regarding the issue they have come to discuss.

Often a client will need to use the bathroom when they arrive if they have been travelling, and it is important to have this room close to your consultation room. If your situation allows, it is preferable that your client does not have to go through areas of your home or office being used by others.

b) Internal State of Mind

Your own state of mind is most important to the successful outcome of the reading. A calm and relaxed state of mind is absolutely essential.

If you are anxious, agitated, stressed, or too tired then you cannot offer your best. Likewise if you are feeling defensive about what your client might think or concerned about how your insights will be received, then the way in which you communicate will be affected, and your self-focused concern reduces your ability to focus on your client.

In real life we find that most consultants have some concerns or tendency to react in particular ways which can create a bias. Self knowledge and awareness, plus the willingness to face this and prepare for the consultation will reduce any negative contribution.

Your own experiences in personal growth and development will provide fertile ground for understanding some of the processes your client may be going through. It is important that you are genuine in your own search for growth and fulfilment.

Your experiences may also provide your biggest blocks in understanding the internal processes of your client if you believe these are the only or even the best answers. Conducting consultations for people requires a real willingness to enter their world without judgement, and a willingness to get a feel for their perspective.

What has assisted you in your life may not assist others. Their needs may be quite different. Part of your work is to understand their needs.

Your greatest asset will be your capacity to listen....to really listen. However you cannot listen to another if you desperately need to be heard yourself. This will be a one way consultation.

When someone feels really listened to there is a remarkable energy exchange that provides a deep stillness in both the client and the consultant. No more words are needed. This moment has real meaning. It is timeless and sacred.

3.   The Arrival of the Client

Welcome your client. From the moment that your client arrives at the front door of your office or home, it is important that they feel welcome. It is also important that the client feels safe and comfortable.

If this is not the case then your capacity to establish an open relationship in an atmosphere of mutual trust may be impaired.

4.   The Warm up Phase

The importance of this phase is easily overlooked by many consultants. By this time you should both be relaxed and seated comfortably. Small talk about the weather and about who referred them to the reading is a fine way to take your client's mind away from their other preoccupations.

You can now begin by explaining a few basics about what palmistry is all about, and speak a little about your special areas of focus should you have any. This is an excellent time to remind your client about what you do and what they can expect from the reading.

On rare occasions you may find that in spite of all that you have previously said, your client has not really listened and has come with a different expectation of what they will receive in the reading. This is an opportunity to terminate the reading or re-negotiate if they are not happy to pay for what you are really offering.

If everything has in fact gone smoothly, your client will hopefully be more relaxed and open to receive what you have to offer.

This preamble should have the effect of settling your client's mind, especially if they have come in from busy traffic and a hectic lifestyle. Now is a good time to encourage your client to talk about any particular needs or wishes they may have, and to confirm that which you are offering is what they are expecting from the reading.

5.   The Exploration Phase

(a) Your First Impression:

The first thing to look for is the overall appearance of the hands. What is your gut reaction and your intuitive feeling or impression of the hands?

Do they look agile, energetic, heavy and lifeless, powerful, or something else. Do they remind you of something? Or give you a certain feeling? Try to name it, at least in your own mind.

This is not something that can be learnt out of a book, nor is it something particularly "psychic". It's really just about naming the obvious, describing some of the basic characteristics or impressions that register in your mind. People appreciate basic truths that are presented in an objective and respectful way.

Ask your client to hold out their hands above the table for a moment. Permit them to present the hands palms up or down, any way they like.

Their hands will have a certain expression. This may be open, closed, grasping, or warm. Even though we must make allowances for self-consciousness, the hands will speak in their own way.

The hands are a dynamic expression of life.....the life of your client. Their expression is not static or fixed, but is continually in a state of flux. The hands record and express the life energy of your client

Take note. Observe.

(b) The Analysis:

This is your assessment and interpretation of the shape and qualities of the hands of your client. This has already been covered in this book.

6.   The Discovery of the Underlying Disturbance

This phase emerges somewhere in the previous phase. This is when you discover the real reason why your client is consulting you - you discover what is really disturbing them. Often, for example, a client will be seeking clarification about career direction or some relationship issue, and you are able to establish that what really leads them to the question is some underlying unhappiness or unfulfilled need. It can sometimes be something quite simple. For example unhappiness in a relationship may come about because of boredom or frustration in other areas. If these other needs are remedied then the relationship may easily be re-kindled.

It is important to look beneath the surface and seek the underlying reason why your client is seeking advice. Very often your client has not looked any deeper themselves.

7.   The Jolt of Insight:

This phase in the process of a reading does not always take place - it depends on a number of factors including why the person is really there, how open they are, and their own state of self awareness.

The jolt of insight comes when the client suddenly realizes and understands the underlying reason for their questions, and sees things in a new and revealing light. Sometimes this is not so much a jolt as the slow dawning of understanding. It can be something as simple as realising that there is no need for guilt about a particular issue, or finally understanding the real impact of a past event. This can be a very healing time for your client and needs to be treated with all the reverence it deserves.

8.   The Understanding Phase

This is the time of putting everything into perspective, and sometimes about going over other questions that were previously raised and can now be connected with their new insight. This is often a good time to encourage your client to talk more about their future intentions in the light of which they have discovered.

9. Wrap Up and Summary

This is the time to link all the things you have discussed together and to summarize what has been said. The effect of this is put things into perspective for your client, and to prepare them for the finish of the reading. This is a time for any final questions. Some readers have difficulty knowing when and how to stop, and it is possible to overload your client with too much information than is necessary.

By doing a summary and indicating that this is the time for final questions you can proceed smoothly to the completion. This is also the time to bring up the question of payment if you did not ask the client to pay before the reading.

Some beginning consultants feel embarrassed or awkward about asking for money. However the client has agreed to pay and you deserve to be paid. It is important to be clear and confident with your request for payment. You are a professional consultant providing a professional service.

Answers to questions to test your understanding
at the end of lessons 2- 28

Lesson 2: Historical Context & Terminology
1. False. 2. True. 3. False. 4. True.

Lesson 3: The importance of Context
1. False. 2. True. 3. False. 4. False. 5. False.

Lesson 4: Which Hand do I read?
1. True. 2. True. 3. False. 4. False. 5. True.

Lesson 5: Hand Structure
1. False. 2. True. 3. True. 4. True. 5. False.

Lesson 6: Palm Dimensions
1. False. 2. True. 3. True. 4. True. 5. True.

Lesson 7: Finger length and Outline
1. True. 2. False. 3. True. 4. False. 5. True.

Lesson 8: Hand shape: Combining palm and fingers
1. False. 2. False. 3. True. 6. True.

Lesson 9: Finger tips
1. True. 2. False. 3. False. 4. True. 5. True. 6. False.

Lesson 10: Additional features relating to hand structure
1. True. 2. False. 3. False. 4. True. 5. True. 6. False.

Lesson 11: The zones of the palm
1. True. 2. False. 3. True. 4. True. 5. True. 6. False.

Lesson 12: The fingers
1: Venus and Mercury. 2: No. 3: Ego. 4: Outer side of the hand. 5. Yes. 6. No.

Lesson 13: Measuring & interpreting the fingers and thumb
1: True. 2: False. 3: False. 4. False. 5. True.

Lesson14: The Nails
1: False. 2: True. 3: True. 4. True.

Lesson 15: Finger Sections
1: True. 2: False. 3: True. 4. True. 5. False.

Lesson 16: Finger Lean
1: True. 2: False. 3: True. 4. True.

Lesson 17: The thumb
1: True. 2: False. 3: True. 4. True.

Lesson 18: The lines in general
1: True. 2: False. 3: True. 4. False. 5. True.

Lesson 19: The Life Line
1: True. 2: True. 3: False. 4. False. 5. True.

Lesson 20: The Head Line
1: False. 2: True. 3: True. 4. False. 5. False.

Lesson 21: The Heart Line
1: False. 2: True. 3: False. 4. True. 5. False.

Lesson 22: The Combination Line
1: True. 2: False. 3: True. 4. False. 5. True.

Lesson 23: The Saturn Line
1: True. 2: False. 3: True. 4. False. 5. True.

Lesson 24: Branches from the Main Lines
1: True. 2: False. 3: True. 4. False. 5. True.

Lesson 25: The Secondary Lines
1: False. 2: True. 3: True. 4. True. 5. False.

Lesson 26: Incidental Markings
1: False. 2: True. 3: False. 4. True.

Lesson 27: Hand Types
1: False. 2: False. 3: True. 4. False. 5. True. 6. False.

Lesson 28: Dermatoglyphics
1: True. 2: False. 3: True. 4. True.

About the Author

Peter Burns began reading palms, and consulting and teaching palmistry in 1984. He spent seven years consulting at the Fremantle markets in Western Australia seeing approximately 1500 people each year. He has lectured and conducted many teaching seminars in Australia and has also lectured in the USA and Canada.

His extensive research of the literature on palmistry revealed a number of basic errors which have been perpetuated over many decades. When corrected, profound psychological insights can be obtained from reading the hands. For therapists and healers these insights provide invaluable assistance for the care and assistance of clients.

Also an active as a astrological consultant and teacher of astrology, Peter holds the Federation of Australian Astrologers Diploma and is recognized as a Horary Craftsman through the Frawley Apprenticeship in Horary Astrology. From 2006 through 2008, Peter served as president of the Victorian Astrologers Association and is editor of the quarterly national *Journal of The Federation of Australian Astrologers* since 2000. He has also been been a regular guest speaker on ABC radio in WA and on 3RRR in Melbourne Australia.

Currently Peter focuses on teaching palmistry and astrology through his distance education courses through the Ambrosia Academy of Astrology. See details on *www.ambrosiaastrology.com*.

Other Publications by Peter Burns

Peter has been the national editor of the quarterly ***Journal*** for the Federation of Australian Astrologers (FAA) since 2000 and has published numerous articles in the ***Horizons Newsletter*** for the Victorian Astrologers Association, the Australian ***Wellbeing*** magazine.

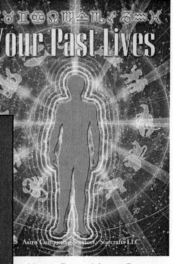
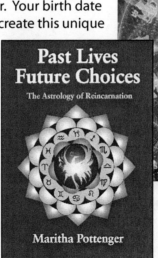

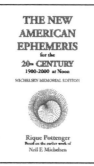

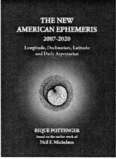
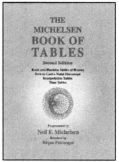
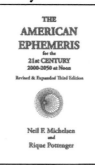

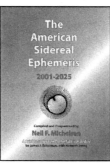
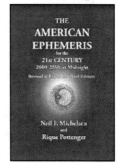

Personalized Astrology Lessons

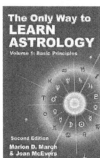
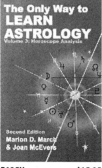

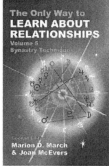
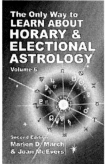
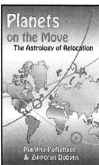

Also from Starcrafts LLC
Imprints: *Starcrafts Publishing, ACS Publications*

All About Astrology, a series of booklets by various authors

The American Atlas, Expanded 5th Edition, Thomas G. Shanks

The American Ephemeris 1950-2050 [at Noon or at Midnight],
Trans-Century Edition, by Neil F. Michelsen and Rique Pottenger

The American Ephemeris for the 21st Century 2000-2050 [at Noon or at Midnight],
Revised & Expanded Third Edition, Neil F. Michelsen and Rique Pottenger

The American Heliocentric Ephemeris 2001-2050, Neil F. Michelsen

The American Sidereal Ephemeris 2001-2025, Neil F. Michelsen

The Asteroid Ephemeris 1900-2050, Rique Pottenger with Neil F. Michelsen

Astrology for the Light Side of the Brain, Kim Rogers-Gallagher)

Astrology for the Light Side of the Future, Kim Rogers-Gallagher)

Astrology: the Next Step, Maritha Pottenger

Astrology and Weight Control, Beverly Ann Flynn

The Book of Jupiter, Marilyn Waram

Dial Detective, Revised Second Edition, Maria Kay Simms

Easy Astrology Guide, Maritha Pottenger

Easy Tarot Guide, Marcia Masino

Future Signs, Maria Kay Simms

The International Atlas, Revised 6th Edition, Thomas G. Shanks & Rique Pottenger

The Michelsen Book of Tables, Neil F. Michelsen

Moon Tides, Soul Passages, Maria Kay Simms, with software CD by Rique Pottenger

The New American Ephemeris for the 20th Century, 1900-2000, at Midnight
Michelsen Memorial Edition, Rique Pottenger, based on Michelsen

The New American Ephemeris for the 20th Century, 1900-2000, at Noon
Michelsen Memorial Edition, Rique Pottenger, based on Michelsen

The New American Ephemeris for the 21st Century, 2000-2100 at Midnight
Michelsen Memorial Edition, Rique Pottenger, based on Michelsen

The New American Ephemeris for the 21st Century, 2007-2020:
Longitude, Declination, Latitude & Daily Aspectarian,
Rique Pottenger, based on Michelsen

The New American Midpoint Ephemeris 2007-2020,
Rique Pottenger, based on Michelsen

The Only Way to Learn Astrology, Volumes. 1-6 series
Marion D. March & Joan McEvers

Past Lives, Future Choices, Maritha Pottenger

Pathways to Success, Gayle Geffner

Planetary Heredity, Michel Gauquelin

Planets on the Move, Maritha Pottenger and Zipporah Dobyns, Ph.D.

Psychology of the Planets, Francoise Gauquelin

Spirit Guides, Iris Belhayes

Tables of Planetary Phenomena, Third Edition, Neil F. Michelsen

Unveiling Your Future, Maritha Pottenger and Zipporah Dobyns, Ph.D.

Yankee Doodle Discord: A Walk with Eris through USA History, Thomas Canfield

Your Magical Child, Maria Kay Simms

Your Starway to Love, Maritha Pottenger

CPSIA information can be obtained at www.ICGtesting.com
Printed in the USA
BVOW080038250512

291055BV00002B/1/P

9 781934 976340